A GUIDEBOOK FOR A NEW HUMANITY

David Lane

A GUIDEBOOK FOR A NEW HUMANITY

Awakening Your Higher Consciousness

Awaken

Copyright © 2018 by David Lane

All rights reserved. No part of this book may be reproduced, stored in a retrieval system or transmitted, in any form or by any means, without the prior written consent of the publisher, except in the case of brief quotations, embodied in reviews and articles.

Awaken
Perth, Western Australia
www.davidlane.net.au

ISBN 978-0-9952665-7-5 (paperback)
ISBN 978-0-9952665-8-2 (ebook)

Produced by Page Two
www.pagetwostrategies.com
Cover design by Elisa Gutiérrez & Peter Cocking
Interior design by Peter Cocking
Printed and bound in the United States of America

18 19 20 21 22   5 4 3 2 1

Contents

Preface 1
Acknowledgements 3
A New Paradigm 5

1. God the Divine 7
2. The Truth 21
3. The Birth of God 31
4. Energy and the Creative Process 49
5. The Brain 87
6. Raising Our Consciousness 105
7. Levels of the Mind 117
8. Universal Mind 139
9. The Blueprint 147
10. Images and the Higher Self Mask 157
11. Moving Through the Third Dimension 169
12. The God State 181

Conclusion 187
Resources 188

Preface

THE DESIRE to write this book was driven by a new understanding that evolved out of a lifetime of seeking common denominators between a broad spectrum of information on how God came into existence, what God is, and how God operates. I also wanted to share the big picture of what I have discovered on my spiritual journey. This book is the result of more than thirty years of commitment to the path and of finding answers that made sense to me. These answers came from years of reading, studying, attending workshops, and applying a diverse range of information to my life to see what worked.

I was very confused about God and the purpose of life during my earlier years, and this created a lot of frustration and unhappiness for me. I wanted answers that uncovered the higher purpose of my life. I was brought up believing that I needed an intermediary (in other words, a priest or spiritual guru) who had the answers and would enable me to contact

God "out there." My most enlightening discovery was that I already had everything I needed "within," where I had direct contact with my maker. I did not need anyone else for guidance because all the answers were inside of me. All I needed was the awareness of how to uncover, understand, and apply them to life. This is true of everyone! Life works for me now, and most importantly, it makes sense. I understand myself and my life's purpose.

My intention is to present a comprehensive model of the purpose of life plus lay out the general path towards enlightenment and provide tools and markers to help people on their journey. I am sharing this story to inspire you to find the very *unique purpose* of *your own journey*. It is yours to discover, and your divine self will guide you all the way if you let it.

Acknowledgements

THERE HAVE been so many people, books, and teachings that have influenced my journey that led to writing this book. They have come from all walks of life and belief systems, from ageless wisdom to modern science (quantum physics).

One person who has had an impact on the information in this book is my friend David Ford. David's diverse knowledge of the various teachings of mainstream religions has provided a wonderful and very necessary cross-check on the occasionally challenging concepts that have emerged from my research. The countless hours of discussion have helped us both broaden our understanding of the higher purposes of life and creation itself. We pursued many differences and contradictions until we found common ground. I also owe Janice Lwin a big thank you for the significant contribution that she made towards getting this book started. The talents of both of you are greatly appreciated. Finally, Dr. Calista Benz influenced the presentation and order of the information provided, because of her generous offer to review the manuscript.

I also want to thank all the people who gave me feedback on my first book, *The Handbook to Heaven*. Your positive observations gave me the confirmation and confidence that I was on the right track. I would not have tackled this project without such input.

The world is a better place because of all of you.

A New Paradigm

. . . .

TO LET the new in, we need to let the old go. This does not mean that we disregard everything that has gone before. Human consciousness has come a long way and we have experienced much fear, pain, confusion, love, happiness, and wisdom along the way. We have learnt so much in some areas and have learnt so little in others. Humanity basically understands that we can live in peace and harmony but, in the main, this understanding remains merely a concept. We don't apply these principles and put them into practice. There is something so fundamentally wrong that we are in danger of destroying ourselves; meanwhile, we are on the brink of creating a major positive shift in consciousness about who we are and our higher purpose.

Science and technology are testimonies to the brilliance of the human mind. However, we've struggled to keep up with the exploration of our spiritual side. It is as though we have almost forgotten about the importance of our relationship with each other and creation itself as we continue our pursuit of materialism and the control of our environment. We need to reverse this trend, and can do so by uniting the more subjective approach of spiritual teachings and the very objective approach of science, to understand the higher truths of creation. There are many parallels between scientific research and spiritual truths and we need to bridge the gap.

This book provides information about the process of creation and the processes that God uses to support, communicate, and send information to all that has been created. It also offers a somewhat unusual model of how humans spiritually evolve. These two parts have been melded into one concept that has the potential to pave the way for a new paradigm. This paradigm provides information on how we can evolve our consciousness by first understanding how we arrived at this level and then how we can evolve to the next level.

This book will explore some of the main higher truths found in both religion and science, plus their relevance to human consciousness. It will also give some basic guidelines for those who want to make the hard, but hugely rewarding, adjustments required to attain higher consciousness. A new paradigm that will supersede the old one is emerging—a new humanity and a new level of consciousness will replace what has been. We will find and live the Divine within instead of our lives being an expression of a fragmented spirit. Love and unity will replace fear-based separation and individuality.

I
God the Divine

. . . .

Inside each of us is the pure essence of the Divine.

THE JOURNEY towards understanding who we are and our connection to God starts by understanding the energy of creation. It makes sense that there is ultimately only one source that started creation. It is beyond our comprehension to perceive the power of this source, which is commonly known as God or sometimes referred to as the "Supreme Being," "I AM Presence," and "Super Consciousness."

RELIGIONS AND SCIENCE

Religions traditionally have had a monopoly on being the authority on God. However, science is challenging the more subjective beliefs of religion with an empirical approach to what God is and how this energy operates, with scientific research providing understanding that confirms some of the greatest religious concepts about God and creation. Science provides very credible information that supports the highest truths. Some of this information will be explored throughout the book. When religious teaching and scientific research describe the same thing from a different perspective, the credibility of that subject increases. This is happening more often since the introduction of quantum physics and evidence of these common denominators shows up throughout this book.

God

God is sometimes described as the "I AM" presence, which is a form of energy or consciousness. The understanding of what this means will develop as different concepts unfold. The starting point is that God is at the top of the hierarchy of creation as we know it. It is described as "all that exists" or "all that is." There are two aspects of God that are responsible for creating consciousness and maintaining life. The "Creator" is the masculine aspect of God. The Creator uses the creative energy, or the "creative force," to manifest the universes. The "Heart" is the *feminine* aspect of God that sustains life. This energy is called the "life force." When these two energies come together, we have manifested life. We can come to know about God by exploring these two aspects.

Everything is a form of energy and of consciousness that has life force flowing through it. For example, humans are a form of consciousness that have life force flowing through us. This life force gives us animate life. If our life force stops flowing, our human form of consciousness cannot be sustained and we die. Our bodies decay and return back to their original forms of energy, which began in the earth. (Our spirit and higher self exist on much higher vibrations and so are not affected by the specific vibrations associated with the life force that gives humans life.)

The Mind of the Creator Creates Consciousness

Consciousness is a form of energy. This creative energy generated by the Creator's mind is called the "creative force." All forms of creation are manifested forms of consciousness that started in the mind of the Creator. The Creator also made the "universal mind," which is separate from the Creator's mind, though the two are closely aligned. The Creator can access the universal mind but the universal mind cannot affect the mind of the Creator. All of creation has access to the universal mind. This means that all parts of creation have the potential to communicate with and affect any other part of creation through the universal mind, but they cannot affect the Creator.

The Universal Mind

Everything in creation uses this one mind, the universal mind. There are no individual minds! It may be hard for many people to grasp the concept that there is only one universal mind, because we are so accustomed to thinking that we are individuals with minds of our own. There are several levels to the mind, and this will be explored in later chapters. The mind facilitates all levels of consciousness; however, access to its different levels depends on the vibration of the consciousness that is using it. The Creator only needs to access the highest level, while discrete aspects of the universal mind access different levels of consciousness, depending on the qualities of consciousness involved. In some parts of this book, I will refer to the universal mind as "your" or "our" mind. Whatever the case may be, it is still the same mind being accessed. It needs to be emphasized that we don't have a mind but we access the universal mind to function as human beings.

Matter is a form of creation; therefore, it has consciousness. It may be a little easier to understand how this universal mind affects the formation of matter if we look at how the structures of human cells are formed. These cells depend upon their respective DNA compositions for their specific structures and functions. The strands of DNA contain chromosomes that hold the codes/information for all the potentials of the cells. The makeup and function of each cell depends on which chromosomes, or codes, are switched on/activated and which ones are switched off/deactivated. The original makeup of the cell DNA that we were born with can change. The information that determines which codes are active and which ones are not enters the cell from its environment. Much of this information is due to the energy generated by the thoughts from our mind. In other words, the mind has a major influence on changes to the structure and makeup of a cell.

Just like the life and purpose of each human cell, the purpose, structure, and function of matter exist because of the incoming information that governs it. If we could trace the information and codes that control creation back to its source, then we would find energy being generated from a mind. Instead of a localized part of the mind that we call a human mind, it would come from the universal mind, and the universal mind is a hologram of the Creator's mind. The ability of a human to affect and control outcomes is based on the same ability as that of the Creator. However, our ability is minuscule when compared with the power generated by the Creator's mind. This replication of the same ability is an illustration of the great spiritual principle of "as it is above, so it is below." The hologram represents this same principle in action.

The Heart of God Continuously Generates the Life Force Energy

Creations are sustained by the life force energy, or the essence of life. This is a different energy than the creative force that generates all the different forms of consciousness. It is the flow of energy that is required to sustain life and, therefore, it is called the life force. There is a continuous supply of energy that flows out from the heart of God. The human heart is a hologram of the heart of God. It pumps blood throughout the body and blood is responsible for supplying the life force to our bodies. If our heart stops, then our life ceases and our body starts to breakdown. The heart of God pumps the life force throughout creation. This energy gives life to all that has been created and then the continuous flow sustains that life. If God stopped the flow, then all life would cease; creation would be lifeless and start to break down.

Once energy is created it lasts forever, so what happens to creation if the energy supply (life force) is turned off? It would eventually return to the original form that existed in its pre-creative state. This pre-creative form may be almost nothing. (Some scientific theories suggest that all the matter in the universe could be condensed into something smaller than an atom.)

It makes sense that if God can stop the flow of life at any given moment, then It can also change anything at any time.[1] If God did not want any part of creation to exist, then It would switch off the life force to it. The human race may seem like a failed project from our perspective, given that it perpetually lives in fear and disharmony. However, according to some information that comes from very high levels of consciousness, human life is said to be a grand experiment and experience. There is nothing negative about any part of creation when viewed and understood from the highest planes of consciousness.

---

[1] I refer to God as "It" because It is a masculine and feminine, all-encompassing omni-energy, and I do not know of another suitable pronoun for this entity. I capitalize "It" as a mark of respect. No one can see God. We can only experience Its energy or presence.

In short, we are ultimately an "I AM" energy and connected to God's I AM energy. Our I AM energy is totally separate from the mind and does not need to use the mind to connect to the higher energy of God. The mind actually gets in the way of this connection. We cannot connect to God through the mind because the universal mind is separate from the mind of the Creator (as was previously explained). Anyone familiar with deeper meditation knows that we have to still the mind (stop using it) to be with God.

The universe is made up of many forms of energy; therefore, we can come to know a part of the Creator by understanding the universe and the universal laws that govern it. These laws are the same principles that the Creator uses to create and sustain life. Here are some principles of universal energy:

1. All creation is a form of energy.
2. Once energy is created it lasts forever.
3. All energy can be measured by its level of vibration.
4. Energy can change shape, form, and vibration.
5. Energy is always moving.
6. Energy naturally moves in cycles.
7. All energy will return to its point of generation.
8. Creation is a process.
9. All creation exists as a hologram.
10. The universe and all within the universe are subject to the universal laws.
11. The greatest universal law is the law of balance.

Let's now look at these principles in more detail.

1. All Creation Is a Form of Energy.

If something exists, then it is a form of energy. This includes everything from the densest forms of matter through to the highest vibrating etheric forms that exist above and outside our reality. Everything in existence is a part of a "Oneness" that is like a kaleidoscope. Any small and seemingly insignificant change in any part of the pattern will have an effect on the whole. Change often happens at such a slow and subtle rate that we don't see it happening. We often don't realize it is happening until we see the result of the change. However, energy is always moving and change is always happening.

2. Once Energy Is Created It Lasts Forever.

We cannot destroy energy; we can only change its form. This point is very important for understanding how we deal with negative energies and thought patterns. We can create positive energies and thought patterns to counteract and even override negative energies. A positive energy may be able to neutralize or reverse the effect of a negative energy—but not eradicate it. We can change the form of a negative thought pattern by transmuting it into a more positive one. We can also change the form of matter, transforming it by changing its vibrations. However, we are changing the form and not the existence of the energy itself.

3. All Energy Can Be Measured by Its Level of Vibration.

Because consciousness and energy are interconnected, all consciousness has a measurable vibration. Human consciousness generates energy, and our level of awareness can be measured by the vibrations our consciousness generates. For example, we can monitor how we *feel* when we are having positive thoughts versus when we are having negative ones. Positive feelings are lighter, because they are the result of higher vibrations. Negative feelings are heavier, because they are a result of lower, denser vibrations. Our level of awareness also governs and reflects our consciousness, thoughts, and spiritual evolution.

4. Energy Can Change Shape, Form, and Vibration.

We have the ability to transmute low vibrations into high ones. We can also change the density of certain forms of matter, which are also forms of energy. For example, we can change water into steam by boiling it or into ice by freezing it. This is a good analogy for how we can have different forms of the same energy. One and the same as energy, the three different states of the water transform but never cease to exist.

Let's take the life cycle of a tree as another example. The seed of a tree holds all the information/codes of the potential structure of the tree. The seed germinates and the potential of its form is activated. The seed becomes a seedling and eventually grows into a mature tree. The minerals and nutrients in the soil, as well, contribute to the building blocks that form the tree. It is easy to see, however, that the form of the tree is very different from the matter that helps create it. It is the "creative codes" originally held in the seed that govern the process. The potential held in the seed remains dormant until the seed's germination is activated by water. Then, life force is activated, the seed comes to life, and the life force remains for the life span of the tree.

5. Energy Is Always Moving.

If it did not move, then it would not exist. Energy is moving towards either the negative or the positive. This is a major concept for understanding how we influence our spiritual journey through life on earth into the higher planes of consciousness. Some people believe that they are in a neutral state when not doing anything. It is necessary to rest to enable our body to re-energize. However, we need to get active again as soon as we have recharged because inactivity creates decay. There is a common truism that "If you don't use it, you lose it." Be aware that if you are not moving towards the positive, then you must be moving towards the negative. Some movements in either direction may be obvious, while others are so sublime that we do not notice them. However, they are happening all the time. Every hour and every minute.

If you are not creating a positive state, then you can be certain that you are moving towards the negative. If any part of your body is not in homeostasis (a state of health), then it is in a state of decay. If we are lazy in any area of our life, then part of us is going backwards. If any part of our body is not being used, then the body naturally stops supplying energy to it. This creates the negative state of decay. This does not mean that we have to be using every part of us all the time, because that would be impossible. However, we need to be aware that what we don't use will deteriorate. The same is true of our spiritual growth. We must keep moving towards the positive, otherwise we will slowly slide towards the negative. The further we slide, the harder it is to return to where we were.

6. Energy Naturally Moves in Cycles.

A fine example of this is the orbit of the earth. Our planet moves around the sun in 365 days, just as the moon orbits the earth in approximately twenty-seven days. Each revolution is one cycle. But, for example, a tree's life cycle is more complex, because it involves several sub-cycles. The seed is the main instigator of the process because it holds all the information codes necessary for the tree to reach its potential. Other essential factors are involved: the nutrients and minerals in the soil; the water that triggers germination and sustains life. Light provided by the sun facilitates photosynthesis, which also helps generate growth and sustain life. In fact, everything associated with the life of the tree has its own cycle that consists of a beginning, a middle, and an end. Everything in existence, from thoughts to the universe, will complete this same three-stage cycle.

7. All Energy Will Return to Its Point of Generation.

In spiritual terms this means that, because the Creator created everything, all will return to its point of creation, which is at oneness with the Creator. There are differences in how long an individual cycle is, the directions it takes, and the experiences that occur during a unique cycle. An individual cycle could last a split second or millions of years or anything in between. The human race and the individuals within it have a lot of control over how long they will take to pass through the earth plane of experience (the third dimension) on their way back to the oneness of the Creator. Once our consciousness attains a certain higher level, our vibration causes us to move to higher planes of consciousness and experience. These will also be a part of our cycle as we continue on our way back to our starting point with the Creator.

8. Creation Is a Process.

There is a three-stage process by which everything is created: thought, word, and deed. All three stages are needed.

1. *First stage*: This occurs when a thought about something we want to do enters our mind. If we don't do anything else with that thought it will pass and nothing will get done.
2. *Second stage*: At this stage, we give the original thought more energy by thinking or talking about it. We may start planning how we will do something and what the end result will look like. The original thought increases in power as similar energy accrues. There is no time limit on this stage and sometimes ideas get "put on the back burner" until a person feels motivated enough to carry them out.
3. *Third stage*: This is when we put the original thought into action, manifesting the original thought. The final outcome may not be exactly what we originally envisioned because

the second stage may have modified it into a perceived better outcome.

The principle of the three stages applies to all creation, which includes the Creator. Humans have the power to create outcomes because we have powerful minds coupled with incredible brains that work together to produce remarkable results. Everything we have done and will do gets created according to this three-stage process. This understanding is paramount to our evolution to the higher levels of consciousness. It may be very daunting to accept that we have directly or indirectly created everything that happens in our life—no exceptions! Much of this creating happens on a subconscious level, so it is hard to recognize how we're doing it. It may be hard to acknowledge that we create all the negatives in our life; however, with this understanding comes the ability to change the negatives. Acceptance comes before change. How can you change a negative thought pattern if you can't accept that you have it in the first place? But we are also responsible for all the positives in our life—again, without exception.

9. All Creation Exists as a Hologram.

Dr. Bruce Lipton, a well-known and respected American geneticist (see Resources section), has given a great example of a hologram. He explains that a single human cell is a hologram of the entire human body, because it has all the main functions of the human body. It has cardiovascular, immune, digestive, respiratory, nervous, skeletal, and endocrine systems. Just like cells coming together to form a human body, which is a greater consciousness than the individual cell, the combined consciousness of individual humans composes the consciousness of all humanity. In turn, humanity's consciousness is a part of a greater consciousness that combines with other, similar forms of consciousness to eventually get to a point where everything is connected to everything else. We call this mass consciousness, among other names, such as "the oneness" or "all that is."

10. The Universe and All Within the Universe Are Subject to the Universal Laws.

These laws of creation are in perfect alignment with the Creator's intentions. They are also the highest truths. They are the laws that govern how the universe was created and now functions. They were designed to create total and divine synchronicity, synergy, relativity, harmony, and balance. The highest laws of the universe will always encompass the lesser laws associated with them; however, some lesser laws, for example, human-designed laws, may be in conflict with a higher law. If a lesser law is out of alignment with a universal law, then it is not the highest truth. (There are several versions of the universal laws found on the Internet.)

11. The Greatest Universal Law Is the Law of Balance.

When all the other universal laws are in balance, both within themselves and among the other laws, there is divine balance and harmony. This law affects all levels of the holographic universe, from the smallest microorganism to the oneness of the whole universe. If humans could apply the principles of balance to our own lives, then we could attain the harmony so many of us desire. This harmony would spread out to eventually touch the entire human race. Once we find the balance that creates inner harmony and peace, we will be able to observe the phenomenon of balance spreading throughout humanity. Because of the hologram effect, it will also be projected outwards to influence the rest of the universe. There is so much at stake! Information from higher sources tells us that the human race is at a major crossroads, and the direction it chooses to go (positive or negative) will have a rippling effect on the evolution of our entire galaxy.

The law of balance provides us with the greatest measure of how evolved our own consciousness is. When our personal truth is in harmony with the laws of the Creator, there is harmony in our life. Perfect balance equals perfect harmony. Any imbalance in our thinking will create a relative disharmony in an area of our life. All we need to do is look at the parts of our life that are imbalanced, causing negativity and emotional pain, and we will have uncovered an issue to work on. We will know if we are getting back into balance by observing the changes in the associated negative side effects. Any negative thinking will cause an imbalance, no matter how small. As you know from principle six on page 15, energy moves in cycles, including the energy of thoughts. We project either a positive or negative energy out from our energy field. This energy has a more noticeable effect on those close to us and their responses reveal situations for us to experience. We may or may not make the connection between the outgoing and returning energies, but it is there. This is another example of how energy can change form: Our outgoing negative energy transmutes into another form by the receiver's perceptions and belief systems. Their process is personal and it allows for an interpretation unique to them. This is why you may get several different responses to the negative energy that you project outwards, making it very hard, at times, to see the common denominator. However, you can trust that the universal laws will cause your negative energy to return to complete the cycle of what you have generated. The returning energy will in turn create within us a reaction, which may last for a moment or much longer. That reaction is one of the most powerful indicators of the imbalance in your original thinking.

Humans have a huge influence on the imbalance and the associated disharmony of our planet. If we as individuals continue to disregard the universal laws, then we will create imbalance and emotional pain in our life. This imbalance in turn gets generated outwards through our thoughts, and this has a negative effect on humanity and our planet. The imbalance of our planet affects the balance of our galaxy, which creates imbalance in our universe. This is the hologram effect in action. Like the ripples created by throwing a rock into a pond, the negative or positive ripples a person creates with their mind radiates out to have an effect that lessens the farther it travels and mixes with other energies. That is one person. Now imagine the consciousness of all humans as one consciousness that can be very negative or positive and that contributes to the destruction or salvation of our habitat, Mother Earth. Now, instead of a small rock being thrown into the pond to create a little ripple, picture a huge boulder being dropped into the pond. Its waves will wash over the banks and affect a lot more than just the pond. This analogy summarizes how our individual energy accumulates as it combines with that of all other humans, majorly affecting the universe. We have an individual challenge and responsibility to ourselves to learn about the universal laws and bring our consciousness in alignment with them. As a result, we will be contributing to the welfare of the planet and, eventually, the universe. The buck stops with us as individuals!

2

The Truth

. . . .

We are truth seekers.

TRUTH IS a term generally associated with fact or reality. It could be said that the truth is the truth and it does not change. However, our perception of the truth can change. What may be the truth for one person may not be for another. On the surface, these statements can be confusing, because if the truth is the truth, how can it vary? It would be better to say that there are different kinds of truth that fall into three basic categories.

1. The Absolute Truth, or the Undeniable Truth, which Can Be Seen as Fact.
Absolute truths never change. In other words, one plus one equals two. No matter what ever happens in the world, even if we find a more efficient system for addition, one plus one will always make two. It is an undeniable fact. Another simple

example is that the sun always rises in the east and sets in the west. We have undeniable proof of that.

2. Truths That Are Not Absolute and Are Open to Challenge.
Truths that aren't absolute and are open to challenge are influenced by our perceptions and belief systems. This category of truths is accepted as reality until proven otherwise. For example, there was a time when humans believed that the world was flat and that sailing far enough in one direction would cause an explorer to fall off the edge. It may seem absurd now, but people really believed this and many would have argued that it was a fact. It was believed to be real and so in those times it would have been generally categorized as truth associated with fact. However, this belief was proved to be wrong and, therefore, not an absolute truth like most people thought; it was only a perceived truth.

3. Truths That Can Be Seen as Undeniable Fact and That Are Not Absolute.
Believe it or not, a truth that can be seen as undeniable and that is not absolute is that the sun rises in the east and sets in the west. This phenomenon is accepted by nearly everyone as an absolute truth, because in our experience the sun has always done this and, therefore, we believe it always will. But will it? Most people would say yes. However, there is scientific evidence that indicates the earth's rotational speed has slowed to a critical stage, which supports the possibility and prediction that the rotation of the earth could stall. There are ancient myths and records that indicate this happened thousands of years ago. The earth stalled on its rotation and started spinning in the opposite direction. This makes way for the potential that the sun could rise in the west and set in the east. Now we have category one and category two truths encapsulated in

one situation. It is a fact that our short-term, recorded history tells us the sun rises in the east and sets in the west. But it is not a fact that it will continue to do so. This is an example of how many people's personal truths deny the probability of another possibility. We confuse our personal truths with absolute truth. Just because 99.99 percent of the population may believe something is true does not make it an absolute truth.

Personal Truth

So-called truths are not facts or absolute truths; they are what people believe to be the truth. They could be called "personal truths" that describe what a person believes to be the truth. If enough people believe the same thing, then it is likely to be accepted as "the truth," but that truth will always be open to challenge. This challenge often occurs because new information becomes available. Even if this new information is of a higher understanding, it is usually very hard to sway people's minds. Change normally happens slowly, because people generally need time to adjust to a different reality. A new reality such as was presented in the spherical earth scenario can be very threatening to many people's belief systems. The reasons why a new reality can be so threatening are explored in Chapter 5.

Almost everybody understands that one plus one equals two, and it is accepted as the absolute truth. However, many so-called truths are open to interpretation. As such, arguments break out about who is right and who is wrong or if something is true or false. Almost everybody has beliefs that they hold as the absolute truth but that are really only personal truths. The more that their truths are challenged, the more they will defend them. Some people will even fight to the death to defend their truth, because they blindly believe that it is absolute and should never be challenged. We see this frequently in fundamentalist religions.

It is often very hard to introduce a different point of view to influence someone who has been raised under a strict discipline such as a religious one. They are very protective of their beliefs, which they hold absolute. History provides us with many examples of religious conflicts resulting from people trying to spread or protect beliefs that they see as the "right" ones. Many wars have been fought over a principle of "I am right and, therefore, you must be wrong." This misconception is based on a personal truth that is believed to be the absolute truth.

How Personal Truths Are Formed

If we are to evolve our human consciousness to a higher level of understanding, then we need to understand where many of our personal truths originate. Personal truths are associated with our belief systems, which are developed through mind and brain functions. They become our reality. Therefore, it is essential to have some knowledge of how our mind interacts with our brain and its memory to attain a simple but important understanding about how these beliefs develop. We cannot grow to the higher levels of consciousness unless we have the tools to do so. We also need to explore how our bias affects our ability to process any information that is in conflict with our present understanding or personal truth. Why? Because if we want to develop a more comprehensive perspective on how we spiritually evolve, then we need to let go of the belief systems that lock us into any current reality holding us back.

We need to be able to identify the difference between higher truths and personal beliefs. Once we have identified our personal truths, we need to allow other information in, to compare the differences and to see what makes more sense to us. The challenge comes when new information is quite divergent from our old beliefs. Our natural bias will also hinder this process. A part of mastery is the ability to keep an open mind and always be ready to review and compare our truths with others, so that we can seek out the higher truths. Masters do not feel threatened by different points of view for they can keep an open mind. Most people close up when they feel threatened. Closed up and open-minded don't go hand in hand.

Unravelling the Truth
An inbuilt tool that allows us to unravel the truth is the ability to reason. If something does not make sense to us, then we owe it to ourselves to pursue a better understanding. Confusion contaminates the mind. Believing in one thing or its opposite is better than being caught in the middle, where confusion reigns. One of our greatest stumbling blocks to changing is that we identify our self-worth with our beliefs. For example, if someone were to disagree with or criticize our strongest belief, we would be inclined to defend it or take the criticism personally, as if it were a personal attack rather than a point of difference about something we hold as true. We have to separate our self-identity (who we are) and our self-worth (how we feel about our self) to be able to honestly discern what is the truth behind any of our beliefs. Another stumbling block is that our bias automatically leans us towards our belief rather than away from it.

Many people accept information from others who they think have more knowledge. They say things like, "Oh, this person is an authority so they must be right." Even when what is espoused by another doesn't quite fit, many people suppress their inbuilt resources for wisdom. This is one of the main reasons why the majority of people are vulnerable to being controlled and manipulated by a small number at the top. We can only evolve to the higher levels of consciousness once we have learned to listen to our self. Listening to our thoughts is a form of honouring our self. Many so-called gurus have misled followers who never exercise their right to question or disagree. This lack of discernment can be very dangerous.

An Australian Tragedy

A controversial tragedy divided Australia in 1980. The Chamberlain family was camping at a campsite at Uluru (Ayers Rock) in central Australia. They reported that a dingo (a wild Australian dog) took their baby, Azaria, from their tent, saying that they'd left her unattended for a very short time. There was an extensive search but neither the body nor any evidence was found. Suspicions were raised that her mother, Lindy, may have killed the child, mainly because it was almost incomprehensible that a dingo would take a baby. Many people quickly made their minds up and had very strong opinions about what might have happened, and the story was hotly debated in the months that followed. Most Australians very quickly adopted personal opinions about the case, based on very little evidence. Many people, after jumping to the conclusion that she had killed the baby, condemned Lindy. Society formed two opposing sides—one believing of Lindy's guilt and the other her innocence—and both were adamant that their version was the truth. There was very little middle ground. These strong opinions were made on very little evidence and almost no proof at all. Some people still hold on to their beliefs and will defend them, even after thirty years have passed.

This is a great example of how beliefs can become entrenched. Two influencing factors behind the strong response to the Chamberlain family, related to how our brain works, are core beliefs and emotion. One belief was that it was impossible for a dingo to take a baby of Azaria's size. Powerful emotions stimulated by the death of a baby helped embed any associated information (incoming data) into people's long-term memory, where it became people's truth. (This will be explained in Chapter 5.) Because most people don't know how to separate personal truths from real, factual, or absolute truths, their perception of what happened became the absolute truth in their minds and, therefore, unchallengeable. The ensuing opposing arguments that broke out threatened almost everyone's formed opinions, and so more strong emotions were triggered. Anger and hatred soon followed, and then a seemingly full-scale verbal war developed. It is not hard to see how the human race can go to war over differences of opinions. Disagreements can turn into anger, which turns into mistrust and hatred, followed by attack or revenge. The outcome is war.

Lindy was condemned as a murderer by a significant percentage of the population before any investigations or inquests even began. These vindictive, unproven judgements virtually wrecked the Chamberlain family's life. Four years after Lindy was convicted of murder and sentenced to life in prison, an article of Azaria's clothing was found near dingo lairs in the area where the family had been camping. Lindy has now been legally exonerated.

And yet, some people still believe that Lindy murdered her baby, and they will never change their belief because they still have an emotional charge around and some strange investment in believing she's guilty. Even if more compelling evidence could be found to support the dingo scenario, these people have their beliefs locked in—end of story!

As this story shows, belief systems become entrenched in our long-term memory, and once they have a large database, they are almost impossible to change. To be proven wrong is almost inconceivable to some people, and to have a strong core belief proven wrong can easily cause emotional turmoil. This is partly because of our pride and false self-worth and because we identify our self-worth with what we believe.

Our potential is much greater than our beliefs; however, our beliefs can be either our greatest asset or our greatest liability for reaching our potential.

EXERCISE 1: CHALLENGING BELIEFS

This exercise offers one method of challenging your beliefs without having to give them up, presenting a way to reflect on an interaction during which your beliefs are tested. Some people may feel ready to do an overall review of their beliefs; however, it's important to stay grounded during this exercise. It's often extremely unsettling when our strongest, most personal or sacred beliefs are challenged. So, if you try this exercise and feel stressed, uncertain, or confused, then it is likely that the issue you're looking at is too emotionally charged. If you are not consciously aware of what your reaction is about, then it is probably being generated on the subconscious level. Stop, and pick a subject that is less confronting. Once you have mastered this technique with an easy topic, you may be ready to work on a stronger belief. Practise the following steps:

1. Notice when you receive information that is in conflict with something that you believe. For example, you express your opinion about something during a discussion, but someone else offers a conflicting point of view.
2. Observe how you react and see how well you listen to their version of the truth. Does your judgement about who is right and who is wrong interrupt or can you remain calm and open-minded without needing to argue your point? The more charged the subject is for you, the more you are likely to want to defend your truth. Hopefully you can have an amicable and fruitful discussion with the aim of comparing points of view and exchanging ideas.

3. Take the information gained and reflect on it later. Compare your original opinion and see if any new information has broadened your understanding and influenced your belief. There are several questions that you could ask yourself, such as, did you identify your self-worth with your belief? Did you defend your belief as if the other's opposing opinion were a personal attack on you? Did you feel like you won the argument or debate, and if so, did you feel superior? Was your original belief confirmed by the exchange of ideas or do you now have some doubt? Do you feel reassured, content, confused, frustrated, or even angry?

When you practise this exercise, notice how did or would you react if the other started to "lay down the law" about why you are wrong and why they are right? Most people react when told they are wrong. In such situations, it's highly unlikely that you will be able to keep an open mind. You have several options open to you. You could take it personally and feel attacked, although if you react, then you give your power away by allowing another to affect your emotions. The smaller your reaction, the less emotional charge you have around the subject. A balanced person will not overreact, because they will not have any emotional charge present. You could opt to change or end the conversation. Many people think that it's rude to walk away from the conversation, but if you are going to practise loving yourself, you won't accept verbal abuse; accepting another's abuse gives your respect for someone else more importance than your self-respect.

Deciding how you want to be is a big decision. People with powerful self-belief and self-respect will not tolerate being treated badly. Ask yourself this: "Is what I would do the same as what I would like to do?" If not, then which action is stronger or which feels better? Honouring yourself means learning to do what you want to do, rather than what you think you should do. If what you want to do is selfish, then others will see your selfishness. However, sometimes that can be a good thing, because you have exposed a part of you for what it is and self-honesty is paramount if you are striving for self-love. Others might not like your action, but people actually feel safer when they see a true rather than a false person.

You don't have to be right and it is okay to be wrong. If you can admit to yourself that your opinion was wrong, then it probably means that you can change your belief on the subject without much or any internal emotional turmoil. If you believe that the conversation supported your point of view, then say to yourself, "This is the highest truth I have on the subject at the moment, but it may or may not be the highest truth." When you say this, you replace the "right/wrong" model with a model that contains levels of truth. You are also training yourself to think from a new paradigm. All this self-identity is an observation of your lower self, which includes your ego self and spirit self. It is not your true or higher self. (There will be more explanation on the difference in Chapter 10.)

Be aware that your biggest subconscious negative beliefs will be the hardest to uncover and change. This reality will be explored in Chapter 5.

One of the prerequisites for attaining higher levels of consciousness is to be able to let go of the lower levels. This involves being able to keep an open mind to review and change beliefs that no longer serve our climb towards the higher truths. This is not only a challenge: One of the main reasons for being on earth is to evolve into higher consciousness, and this is a personal journey of which we are all capable. No truth is so sacred that it cannot be questioned or tested. The highest truths are found and understood by seeking, questioning, applying, reviewing, understanding to gain wisdom, and keeping an open mind so that other understandings/truths can challenge our current beliefs.

3
The Birth of God

....

How our Creator came to be.

THE NATURE OF GOD

THERE HAS been much written and claimed to be "the truth" about God, what or who God is, and how God operates. A common denominator tends to run through most versions. It supports the belief that is there is ultimately one God who creates all that exists. Science generally avoids any reference to God or a super-consciousness that creates and controls life. Religions use a more subjective approach, whereas science seeks objective proof—hence, the concept of God or a Creator does not suit the scientific approach. There has been a deep divide between religion and science for many centuries. Some religious groups contributed to this divide by shunning the early scientists, calling them charlatans and heretics, and persecuting some of them. Science prevailed through criticism, and aspects of its research have ironically given credence to some of the greatest spiritual teachings.

As we discussed in Chapter 1, the scientific understanding of how the hologram works supports the spiritual teaching of "As it is above, so it is below." A hologram describes, in part, how the smallest part of any whole has the same characteristics and functions as the whole. This means that there is a direct correlation between the characteristics and functions of a single cell with that of the universe, and science can provide objective evidence that this is so. "As it is above, so it is below" is the spiritual, subjective description of the same phenomenon. One of the great contributions of science now concerns the understanding of the Creator as an objective reality, supporting subjective concepts that spiritual teachings provide.

Bringing spiritual concepts and scientific research together has the potential to create a very exciting future regarding the understanding of who we are, of what our purpose is, and of our connection with God. The human race needs to develop a new paradigm that includes a non-judgemental, open mind that enables us to see the higher truths with "new eyes." This does not mean that we discard what we currently believe; however, it does mean that we must apply the tools available to help us open up to new concepts that may be in conflict with what we currently believe. The new paradigm needs to include the tools to compare, renew, and measure new and old information. That may seem like a reasonably easy concept to comprehend, but it can be a very difficult one to apply. In order to put the tools into action, it is beneficial to understand how beliefs are formed and why our perceptions of the world are so heavily influenced by them. How did we acquire them in the first place and why they are so hard to change?

Religions, Spiritual Organizations, and Movements

Religions, spiritual organizations, and movements have the greatest influence over the ways in which many humans choose to relate or not to relate to God. Like everything in creation, these organizations have positive and negative aspects to them. They offer many wonderful concepts on how we should live. Problems arise, however, when religions, organizations, or movements teach that their beliefs about God are so sacred that they cannot be challenged. The danger of this dogma is that it creates a type of "blind faith" wherein the beliefs of the followers are controlled by the hierarchy of the church or organization. This approach does not allow humans to use their God-given gifts of intuition and reason. It interferes with our rights and duty to search for deeper understandings of the Creator and how the Creator operates. Which statement makes more sense to you? "This is the truth and that is the end of it"; or, "This is the truth that we have come to understand so far; however, there may be a better understanding." Hopefully, the latter!

When examining religions from the outside, people often feel puzzled by the different descriptions of God's characteristics and activities and by the respective laws of creation. Some religions believe that these rules are God's commandments. Religious principles are meant to bring the human race together, to live in harmony and peace, plus ideally guide us towards our Creator. Sometimes the interpretations of these principles do the opposite. They create great divisions within society and between different sects and religions. This can be very disheartening, because religions have a lot to offer and have provided us with some wonderful truths and principles by which to live.

Among some religious followers, there also seems to be a misconception that their God needs defending. A lesser God might need defending but God, the Creator of the universes, definitely does not need defending from Its creations. If God did not like an aspect of Its creation, then It could change that aspect into something It did like. For example, if evil was not acceptable, it simply would not be allowed to exist. Everything in creation has a higher purpose and evil is no exception. It is only our inability to understand the big picture that confines us to fearing evil. Evil has its purpose and the more we understand that purpose, the less we will fear it. On the other hand, the more we fear it, the further away our consciousness is from our Creator.

Regardless of how much the human race has advanced its knowledge and awareness, the research and information about the process of creation that science is providing us with is not being readily accepted by many religious followers. The higher truths are found in both institutions if we look. There is something so fundamentally amiss with our approach to this subject that we are in continual conflict and destroying almost all hope of reconciling the differences in pursuit of the truth. People are prepared to kill and die for their beliefs about God and what or who God is. We have got to change if the human race is to survive.

If we are to change, then we have to know what the problems are and how they evolved. No matter what beliefs we hold, no matter what ethnic background we come from, we owe it to the survival of the human race to find truths that bring us together instead of ones that tear us apart. There is no single culture or belief system that can be blamed for the disarray. All hold parts of the higher truths. There are common denominators and we need to explore them with an open mind. The answer doesn't lie in blame or becoming entrenched in beliefs. The answer is much deeper than that, and it already exists, but in order to find it, we need to allow our current beliefs to be scrutinized. We are supported, not condemned, for seeking the higher truths. It is our God-given right to question all information. However, we need to do that with an open heart and mind while using our wisdom. A prerequisite for mastery is applying our own intuition, questioning without judgement, then applying reason and wisdom to seek the highest truths.

No truth is so sacred that it cannot be challenged. To the contrary, the highest truths will always withstand any honest challenge; therefore, it is our duty to seek them out by testing them.

Acceptance for the sake of acceptance and believing for the sake of believing do not reflect a high level of responsibility and consciousness. They reflect someone who is taking the easier path and is not prepared to stand up and take the challenge of mastering their own life. Being responsible brings us closer to God-consciousness, whereas a lack of accountability takes us away.

CREATION

Here is a simplified model of how creation started and continues to function. This version is the result of many years of piecing together all the different information available from religion, spiritual sources, and science.

The Starting Point

There is said to be a consciousness or energy that created the void. Very little is known about this source or if there is anything that lies beyond it.

The Void

A little more is known about this energy. It is an omni-state of consciousness that has not manifested. The void is the source of energy from which creation evolved; therefore, it is also the state of pre-creation. Although existing in an un-manifested state, it holds all the potentials of creation. The ancient

Egyptians believed that there was something before creation. They called it the "state-of-no-state."

The Manifestation of God

The existence of the supreme being was born out of the void. God provided the platform necessary to create life, and this birth was the start of creation as we know it. God is responsible for bringing the potentials of the un-manifested into manifested reality, such as the energy found in life and in the universe. All energy has a starting point, an existence, and an end. Hinduism refers to this God as having three aspects: the creator, the sustainer, and the destroyer of life. (This description aligns with science's understanding of the cycles of energy as having a starting point, a life, and a completion.) The term "destroyer" may imply that God is destructive, so it can be misleading. In this model, I use the term "completion" to mean that a cycle of life has come to an end.

God is described as a triune (three in one) energy because of Its aspects of creation, sustenance, and completion. There is another relevant spiritual teaching that states: "God is Love." Here is another way to try and comprehend God: It is said that everything God has created is a hologram of God. This means that humans must be as well. It may be helpful to understand human consciousness as one expression of God's function.

Human Consciousness

Humans comprise several levels of consciousness. Awareness is a form of energy that has an associated level of consciousness. We access our mind from whatever level of consciousness we are operating on at a given time. What we are aware of in a moment will determine our concurrent level of consciousness. We can be thinking from our ego level (physical self), our spirit level, or our higher self level, but from only one at a time. But, who is the "we" I refer to? We are not our mind, because that is simply a tool we use. We are not our ego, spirit, or higher self, because we can choose to be in any of those states of consciousness. We must be something else! The ultimate truth is that we are a divine essence that can choose to express itself through any level of consciousness that exists below it. We become whatever level of consciousness we think from in a given moment. We know the physical aspect of our humanness, but we also have the ability to leave the physical behind in out-of-body experiences. There is ample evidence of people being able to leave their physical bodies and travel through the higher dimensions. It can be achieved during deep meditations.[1]

God the Creator

God does not have a mind, but the Creator (which is an aspect of God) does. The mind is a tool for the Creator to use. The mind of the Creator generates the energy associated with the many different levels of universal energy, which includes the formation of matter. This energy is known as the "creative force" responsible for generating forms of life and the consciousness that make up our reality. Imagine that certain types of flowing energy are frozen in one place to create a static mass that we call matter. In other words, the creative force brings energy into form. The Creator is the masculine aspect of God. The different expressions of form, such as the human being, are created because of specific codes that control and hold the flowing energy in one static place. Likewise, everything in the

---

1   I have experienced out-of-body travel. During such experiences, I have always been aware of myself and known that I did not have my physical body with me. I was highly conscious and I had control of where I was. I could think and comprehend as normal. If somebody were to have asked me who or what I was while I was in such a state, I would have answered, "I AM" or "I am me."

universe is designed by the Creator with these "creative codes." The Creator also was responsible for the formation of the universal mind, which is separate from the mind of the Creator.

God the Sustainer

The sustaining aspect of God is the "life force" that supplies the energy to preserve form; it gives life to form. It is a continuous flow of consciousness from God that sustains life throughout the universes. If the life force were switched off, then form would return to a state of chaos or no-form. This energy is not the same as the creative force generated by the mind of the Creator. This energy is the feminine aspect of God. The superstring theory provided by science may be describing this energy, or at least a part of it. It is likened to heart energy, which is not the same as the energy created by our mind. Our heart pumps the oxygenated blood through our body to sustain life, so it is also our life force. Likewise, the "heart of God" pumps life force throughout the universe to sustain life. It is important to note that our hearts also produce love-energy and, therefore, we can trust that the heart of God does the same, because we are a hologram of God. Spiritual teachings also state that "God is love" and "the way to God is through love."

The God of Completion

The final stage of the creative cycle describes how all created energy will return to its point of creation. There is no better example of this then the life cycle of a human. We are born (creation); we live (our life is sustained); we die (our life is completed)—and so one cycle on earth is complete. We still exist, but not in the same form. Created life can no longer exist when the life force ceases to flow, and so matter will return to its pre-created state. This is the natural cycle of all energy, and everything is a form of energy. From this perspective, the cessation of our life as we know it is better described as a change of form rather than as death. It is only death to our ego-consciousness; fear of death is often fear of the cessation of our physical self.

Another way to perceive this three-stage cycle is that we evolve out of the oneness to become an individual. We continue in a process that eventually brings us back to the oneness. There are very large and very small cycles, plus countless cycles in between. They are all cycles of energy and are subject to the laws that control energy. A cycle can be a thought, an action, the life span of a fly, or the life span of the universe. All of them are forms of energy that have been created and they will all return to where they started—the point of their creation.

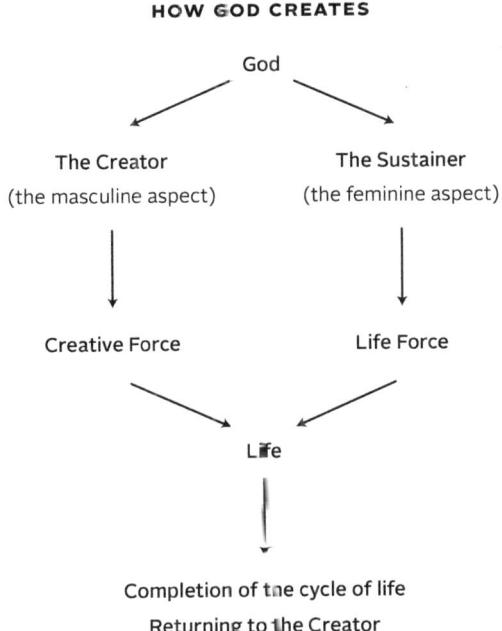

God created humans and we also have the ability to create. However, regardless of how great our potential is, our ability to create is limited by our level of consciousness. A lot of information suggests that we have many of the qualities and potentials of our Creator. One religious teaching refers to humans being created in the likeness of God. Another suggests that we could make a mountain move with faith the size of a mustard seed. We can view these statements from the perspective of the hologram principle, which posits humans as a hologram of God the Creator. It also allows for God to be a hologram of a higher God, or greater force. It may be that a greater God is a hologram of an even greater God and that hierarchy phenomenon keeps reoccurring. Such is beyond the realms of our comprehension, so we can start by understanding our existence as emerging from the void.

Now that we have had a preliminary look at the stages of creation, we will explore them more deeply.

PRE-CREATION AND THE BIRTH OF GOD

Pre-creation

In spiritual terms, the void is called pre-creation, because the first stage of creation occurred when light emerged from the darkness of the void. The energy that exists in pre-creation could be described as a "primal soup," meaning that everything, all potentials, are all mixed together within it. At the present, it's beyond our ability to comprehend pre-creation, but it is believed to exist although we lack the tools to quantify its presence. Words fail us in trying to describe pre-creation, thus we can only say it's unidentifiable and indescribable. Because it's void of light, it could be described as darkness.

The void may be otherwise known as a black hole. Black holes have been described by scientists as incredibly dense and void of light. That description seems to align with qualities of the void's presence. Black hole theory describes, in part, an extremely dense point of existence that eventually pulls in everything in existence. Although it is a controversial perspective, some scientists also theorize that new creations may be born out of black holes. One principle of spiritual evolution is that we evolve back to where we started. Everything that has ever been created will eventually return to its point of origin. In the same way, all of creation will return to the void at some point.

The Birth of God

Some spiritual teachings state that first there was the light, and the light came out of the darkness. There are many references to the light of God. These imply that God is or emits a very bright form of light. It is said that we cannot see God and survive, and this may be because the sheer intensity of the energy is far too great for us to encounter. The description of God's birth is not so different to the flash of light that would have occurred during the big bang about which some science postulates. Regardless of whether science believes that a black hole has intelligence or not, it is relatively easy to believe that the void has intelligence or even a super consciousness. It is almost impossible to believe that God could be born out of something that had no intelligence.

A NOTE ON THE EXPERIENCE OF GOD

Learning about some experiences I had during two very deep meditations may help you to understand the concept of the void and the birth of God. I had set the intention to be taken back to when I first came into existence but didn't know where the intention was going to lead me. During both meditations, I felt puzzled, almost dumbfounded. Then, as often happens, after the experiences I was able to integrate my understanding of them.

The First Meditation

During the first meditation, I found myself in a place that lacked the presence of anything that I could relate to. I knew that I was in a place of nothing and I was waiting for something to happen or to appear that would give some meaning to the meditation, but nothing came. This experience lasted approximately thirty minutes. I was witnessing something, but I can only describe that something as nothing. That sounds like a total contradiction, and under normal circumstances it would be. I could have easily passed this meditation off as a non-event. I only comprehended what I was experiencing much later—it was the void or pre-creation! Upon reflection, there was no light emanating from this place, no colour present. Because of the total lack of colour, "black" seems the best description of this void. There was a sense of it being infinite, with power of an indescribable magnitude. This void was something very dense but penetrable at the same time. It was a denseness that one can be present in and have the sense of being able to move through as well. It seemed to be limited and limitless. To me, it seemed like the ultimate omnipresence. It was everything, all potentials, and nothing at the same time. It was mind-bending to experience all of this at once and felt as something far greater than a third-dimension experience.

In any given moment, people normally have the capacity to experience only little pieces of the whole. Our perceptions are connected to our experiences of the third dimension—which are mainly associated with duality. This makes these perceptions limited, and, therefore, they hinder our ability to see the biggest picture of how the Creator operates. Some spiritual teachings state that when we evolve back to the Oneness, we once again become an omni-state of being, in which all potentials are possible. This omni-state is the same as that of the void or pre-creation experience. The only difference is that the pre-creation state simply is, and there is only a sense of knowing these potentials. Whereas, the Creator has brought that sense of knowing into reality by creating an omnipresence that can be experienced. It is a manifestation of the un-manifested state which has been brought to life. The sense of *nothing* experienced in pre-creation has been manifested into *something* that we can actually experience.

After my experience of this state, I was in mild shock for days as all the pieces coalesced and I realized what I'd been shown.

The Second Meditation

As I began the second meditation, I was shown the void again. I sat in this state for about ten minutes. Then a speck of light appeared and began to move towards me or expand. I recognized that it was in the shape of a *sphere*—the ultimate, perfect shape that underlies all creation as shown in sacred geometry (the five platonic solids). From the sphere, all form evolves. I had first been shown the void and now was witnessing the light evolving out of it. I felt no doubt that the sphere of white light that came out of the darkness eventually intensified to the brilliance and power that we now know as God the Creator, the source of all creation.

On reflection, I realized that I did not witness an entity being formed out of the light—an entity that could be called God. Humans generally have trouble visualizing a God with no form as we know it. I only saw a very bright light being born. This light was consciousness and likely a form of super-consciousness. Interestingly, there are recordings in the bible of a number of visions of God being witnessed. They describe

God as a blinding white light that cannot be seen with the naked eye and that no one can see and survive.

Two More Meditations

These next two meditations were not as powerful as those just mentioned; however, they support the understanding that God is a form that generates a blinding white light. After asking for the highest protection (which I always do before I venture into such uncharted territory), I asked to be shown God. Both meditations came in the form of symbolism, which often happens when I connect with the higher planes of consciousness. I am given the information in symbolic form and its meaning comes to me after the meditation. During the first meditation, I was taken by my guides to a door and was told that God was on the other side. I started to open the door and my mind was immediately shut down at that moment. I was prevented from opening it any farther. I felt myself starting to unravel as the door started to open. It was as though the intensity of the light would have blown my mind apart. I suspect that if I had been naive and hadn't asked for protection, I probably would have borne some dire consequences: We cannot see the face of God and survive. There have been stories of people going into the dangerous area of extremely deep meditation and charred boots being all that is left. It may be that the vibration that they encountered was too high and intense for their physical bodies' cell structure to experience. (We need to use our wisdom when exploring uncharted spiritual territory.)

During the second meditation, the blinding white light was presented to me as shining from behind a hill that obscured it. I remembered the experience of my first attempt to see God, thus I was not going to venture over that hill. It does not really matter if the experience was symbolic or real—I got the message not to venture any farther.

THE ONENESS

Spiritual teachings generally refer to the Oneness as the place we return to when we have evolved back to full awareness or enlightenment. This state of being is also referred to as an omnipresence, meaning that we will have all potentials or none. In other words, we can be whatever we want to be and we can experience whatever we want to once we reach that state of awareness. We could also have several experiences at once. Many religions believe that we will return to our maker. Some in the New Age movement suggest that we will return to the Oneness, which is also God. Some suggest that the highest part of us is God. This may not be entirely accurate.

The Creator is *unlimited*. Recall that God is the source of all Creation. It is the first cause in the creative principle of cause and effect—and the whole of creation is the effect. All Creation is subject to the laws under which it was created, and so its ability to create further is governed by those laws. This makes creation *limited* by the laws that made it. Although we will all return to the Oneness, there will always be a point of difference and separation from God. We were created in the likeness of God, but likeness is not the same thing as being God. It's crucial to understand that we are not God!

As parts of creation, we are subject to its laws. If we want to know how to return to the bliss of the Oneness, there are some basic principles we need to grasp.

THE CREATOR: IMPORTANT PRINCIPLES

The Creator is unlimited in the ability to create, can experience all potentials, and has omnipresence, which gives It the ability to be everywhere at once. This concept is not easy for the human mind to grasp, because we tend to fit everything into separate, easily distinguished boxes. This simplified method of processing information gives us relatively easy reference points with which we can compare and measure. When we perceive things from an omni-perspective, it's like throwing the boxes away. The reference points disappear and nothing is either one or the other anymore. Potential is limitless. True omnipresence can see and experience everything and nothing at the same time. It is not either/or—it is all. Anybody who has evolved to this level of consciousness has the ability to experience many dimensions simultaneously if they choose to. Human experience has been left far behind and they've evolved such that they become their divine self.

Imagine the Creator being like a giant super-computer that can interact with its creations. Now imagine its algorithms can absorb and process billions of pieces of information per nanosecond. It receives much of this information via its feeds, which makes them an integral part of the operation. Humans experience life in the third dimension, and the perceptions of experiences are being sent to the Creator, just like the Internet feeds of the super-computer. Every second, every individual human sends thoughts, emotions, experiences, and perceptions of their experiences across the wires to the Creator. This is one way the Creator chose to experience the life of its creations. Nothing goes unnoticed. There is nothing you believe, think, say, or feel that is not absorbed by the Creator. Every joy, pain, fear, desire, action, and inaction is experienced by the Creator. It is impossible for It not to experience everything that happens.

The earth plane, or third dimension, facilitates the concept of right and wrong, in which judgements are made. It is the plane of polarities that make it possible to experience either one or the other. This is also the plane where beings experience free will and choice. Other dimensions operate differently, without such distinctions. The plane of opposites can only exist if there is separation between the two opposites. The consciousness of the Creator is not judgemental because it is without separation. Everything is one. There is no right or wrong at that level; there is only total understanding and acceptance that everything has its place and has a higher purpose.

4

Energy and the Creative Process

· · · · · · ·

CONSCIOUSNESS OF THE CREATOR

THE MIND of the Creator caused everything in creation to come into being. The universe and all that exists were created by the creative force of this one mind. The creative force underlies all forms of energy or consciousness in the universes. It is the life force that animates consciousness. The fundamental structure and characteristics of the creative force are held in its energy, which is in everything that has been created. Everything in creation is a hologram of the Creator because it is composed of the same energy.

The consciousness of the Creator vibrates at a very high frequency. Although we have the potential to experience this consciousness, it is impossible to measure using our human technology. The higher our vibration becomes, the more closely our personal consciousness aligns with that of the Creator. A basic understanding of the principles of energy, which both affect and are affected by our levels of consciousness, is of importance.

Understanding how energy affects our everyday life will also reveal why our life either works the way we want it to or doesn't. It will also help us understand how we can create the life that we want. It is one thing to *know* that we can change our life and affect other forms of energy with our thoughts, but we usually need a reason for changing. The bigger the change, the profounder the reason needs to be. If we know the principles that underlie how we create outcomes and learn how they work, then we will be better armed to control the process.

Nikola Tesla (1856–1943) was a famous inventor and physicist who had a significant influence on how we understand the workings of energy today. He is reported to have said, "If you wish to understand the Universe, think of energy, frequency and vibration."

Vibration: How We Can Measure Energy

Energy is always moving, towards either the positive or the negative but not in both directions at the same time. Everything in existence, including matter, is a form of energy. There is a correlation between the vibration of matter and its density. The denser the matter is, the lower its vibration. For example, granite is a very dense form of matter and has a low vibration. The higher the vibration, the less dense matter becomes. For example, water is less dense and, therefore, of a higher vibration than granite.

This is important when it comes to understanding the different levels of thought vibration. The more positive a thought is, the higher or lighter its vibration becomes, while the more negative a thought is, the lower and denser its vibration.

There are two characteristics of vibration that are important in relation to our thoughts and the creative process. These are frequency and amplitude. The charts on pages 56 and 57 illustrate these two characteristics.

Frequency

This is the measurement of an energy's number of vibrations over a given period of time, usually per second. The higher the vibration, the more frequent the vibrations per second are, while the lower the vibration, the less frequent the vibrations are per second. Density and frequency are related. For example, sound waves have a higher frequency than water and, therefore, can pass through water. Various spectrums of light all have different levels of vibration. Thought has a very high vibration; however, negative thoughts have a lower vibration than positives thoughts.

EXERCISE 2: SENSING GROUP ENERGY

The next time you enter a room with several people in it, notice what the energy feels like:

1. Does it feel heavy or light?
2. Is it a happy or an unhappy form of energy?
3. Does it have a vibrant charge or does it feel flat?

Remember how it feels and compare it with another experience sometime in the future. Once you draw your attention to this, it is relatively easy to recognize the difference in the energies generated by groups of people. The more negative the energy is, the heavier it feels. The more positive the energy, the lighter it becomes. You don't need science to be able to measure the different energies generated by groups of people once you become aware of your feelings. What exactly are you measuring with your senses? People's thoughts and emotions! The vibrations you're sensing are the combined energy of the thoughts and emotions of all the people present in the group. You can also isolate and identify energy created by smaller groups in the room, if they are having different conversations. Even though the energy created by a smaller group within the whole is contributing to the feeling in the room, the more localized energy will have its own texture. Thus, you can experience how individual vibrations combine to create a collective vibration. Collective vibrations can come together with others to create an even greater combined vibration. In this way, everybody in a community contributes to the community's overall vibration.

As a young man, I occasionally went to the casino. I enjoyed playing the games, although I played very low stakes. I was having a great time and did not feel energetically uncomfortable. The last time I went to a casino, nearly twenty years ago, it had been ten years since my previous visit. I was shocked by how negative and heavy the energy was. I walked around the gambling tables and then left. My awareness had increased over the years and so my vibration was much higher than it had been as a younger man. I later reflected on the energy that I experienced and compared it with the energy I felt at funerals. Although there had been sadness (sometimes extreme) at the funerals, it was coming from a common sharing of grief, support, and friendship. It had a certain quality of life and unity to it, whereas the casino energy felt lifeless. Most people lose at the casino, so I guess the energy is mostly made up of the fear-based negativity of people losing their money. It was a reality check for me and I am a whole lot wiser for the experience.

Vibration and Frequency in Social Gatherings

Energies accrue. You may have heard of the expression "like attracts like," meaning that energies of the same or similar vibration are naturally drawn to one another. Different vibrations can come together by being in the same area, such as a group of people at a family gathering or at a party. An average vibration of the combined energy of the whole group is created. The combining of energies does not stop there. Communities affect societies, societies affect nations. All nations have different vibrations and these combine to create the vibration of humanity. This grand vibration is a measure of the total sum of the combined consciousness expressed by every individual human. No one is left out—we all contribute to this average vibration we call "human consciousness." It's possible to experience the energy of human consciousness on a local level and, if you are aware enough, in ever-larger groups all the way to that generated by the entire human race. The consciousness of individuals affects a group in the same way that the consciousness of distinct nations affects all humanity.

In very relaxed, peaceful states, such as those achieved by meditation, we can experience another type of consciousness. We can tune in to the different vibrations emitted by various forms of nature. For example, we can tune in to the energy (consciousness) of a large, solid rock. The bigger the rock, the more energy it will generate. The vibration of a rock usually feels very slow and incredibly powerful. It's sometimes described as the rock's heartbeat. Some people have experienced the energy of Uluru in central Australia. With a circumference of seven kilometres, this exceptionally large rock generates a very powerful energy. They have described its awesome power as a very spiritually and emotionally moving experience. Such an effect can leave on our personal energy field an imprint that lasts a long time, and the Uluru effect, for some, can be permanent.

AMPLITUDE

Amplitude is what gives energy its impact. If you tap a piece of wood very softly with a hammer, the impact will be low and you are less likely to leave a mark on the wood. If you hit the wood a lot harder, then you will increase the impact and be more likely to leave a mark. If you hit the wood as hard as you can, then the impact may break the wood. This is an example of three levels of amplitude using the same hammer and same wood. The hammer and the wood both have their own vibrations and these do not change, but the force with which they are used creates different levels of impact. This relates to the principle of cause and effect, which will be discussed shortly. Now let's apply this understanding to the power of our thoughts.

Nearly all discrete thoughts will have very little impact on an outcome. When a person repeatedly thinks about the same subject, an accumulation of the same thought-energy will add power to the original thought. The same sort of power will be gained even quicker if more than one person has the same thoughts. By far the greatest increase to the power of thought comes from adding emotion. Therefore, to create powerfully, not only do we need to have positive thoughts, but we also need to trigger strong positive emotions to go with them. If a person believes in what they are thinking, more energy is created. If this energy triggers any emotions, it will create more amplitude. In this way, thoughts and intentions can build into a more powerful form in which there is enough creative energy to generate an intended outcome.

Here is a short list of how thoughts may transform when amplitude is added:

THOUGHT	WITH AMPLITUDE
Interested	Enthusiastic
Enthusiastic	Passionate
Happy	Ecstatic
Keen	Determined or committed
Angry	Raging
Sad	Heartbroken
Uncaring	Totally detached

EXERCISE 3: AMPLITUDE AND CREATING

Reflect on something you wanted to do or create in the past:

1. Did it or didn't it come into fruition? You probably had several thoughts on the subject; otherwise, you would not be able to recall the situation.
2. How determined were you to achieve your goal?
3. Did you lose enthusiasm, or did the excitement build and create more amplitude?
4. If the intention eventually faded into just a memory, was that because of a lack of commitment or enthusiasm, or was it because you realized that it was not a good idea and so not worth pursuing? Perhaps there was another reason, such as not believing in yourself or fear of failure, and so on.
5. If the original idea became a reality, how positive and enthusiastic were you about completing it? Did you overcome any obstacles or was it a relatively easy run?

Reflect on how positive you were during your idea's creation and how much emotion and amplitude were created during the process. It is highly likely that you will be able to recall the presence of both, because each would have had to be there on some level. It would be wise to monitor these two

56 | A GUIDEBOOK FOR A NEW HUMANITY

ingredients the next time you tackle a new idea. The aim is to realize how important amplitude is in the process of creating an outcome from an original thought.

FREQUENCY AND AMPLITUDE OF THE VIBRATION OF ENERGY

All energy is in constant motion and its movement creates vibrations. The charts below show how we can measure two characteristics of energy: the frequency and amplitude of its vibration.

The distance between the waves of vibration is their frequency: The shorter the distance, the higher the frequency and the more positive that energy becomes. The higher the vibration of matter, the lighter matter becomes.

The height of the waves represents the amplitude: The higher the wave, the greater its amplitude.

CHART A

Chart A shows three variations of frequency (distance between each wave) but all have the same amplitude (height).

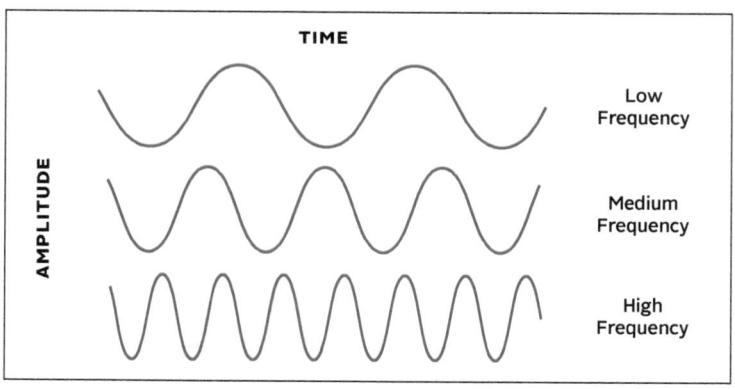

CHART B

Chart B shows two waves with the same frequency but different amplitudes. The greater the distance between the high and low points of the waves, the greater the amplitude.

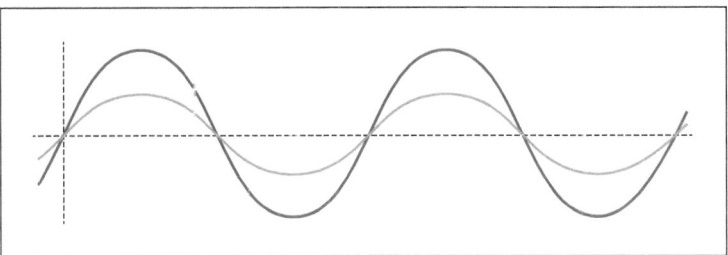

With both waves respectively, the distance between the horizontal mid-line and the highest point is equal to the distance between the mid-line and the lowest point. This illustrates the law of opposite polarities. A positive pole cannot exist without its exact opposite negative pole in the same amplitude. For example, the happier you are, the greater the potential for you to be equally unhappy. (That may come as a surprise to some people but please remember it, as its importance will become evident.) These two principles are also connected to the law of balance.

Balance Creates Harmony

Most people love feeling positive and find it very hard to believe that there is a greater way to live. We all have experienced feeling negative, and who wants more of that? Although being happy is a better way to live than being unhappy, neither is living from the highest truth. Balance brings harmony and inner peace, which is a greater spiritual experience than joy. Happiness may or may not bring inner peace, but inner peace will always bring happiness. Many people, particularly younger people, prefer pleasure to inner peace, because more emotion is created with joy and happiness. Inner peace is the result of the vibrations that bring us into alignment with our Creator. It is not affected by outside forces because it comes purely from within. It does not have the extreme highs that many people enjoy, but it does not have the lows either. It instead has just a beautiful level of serenity that replaces them both.

The more positive you are, the more you create the potential to be negative. (This was demonstrated in the charts on the preceding pages.) This negative potential is also known as resistance. (We will explore the law of least resistance shortly.) This means that more energy is required to remain positive to counter the resistance that is automatically generated at the same time. When your positive amplitude drops down to create a wave that is almost flat, very little resistance is created. Thought vibrations that are aligned with the Creator are almost as flat as the mid-line. Nothing is positive or negative anymore. *Everything just is.* This high level of awareness brings inner peace. Almost no energy is required to remain there, because no resistance is pulling downwards. This is the ultimate state of being in which there are no opposite polarities, such as right or wrong. It is an amazing state, without judgement, because at this level of consciousness all is understood.

An Illustration of Frequency and Amplitude Combined

Another way to illustrate frequency and amplitude is by considering ocean waves breaking on the shore. On most days, a continuous frequency of small, low-amplitude waves break on the beach, with very little effect on the shoreline. But when a storm comes, huge waves break on the same beach, and their impact might dramatically change the shape of the shoreline. The bigger waves will be much farther apart than the smaller waves on the calm days; however, they can do a lot of damage in a very short time—because they have high amplitude, which gives the wave its power, creating a strong impact.

Thought Patterns

Charts A and B could also represent the difference between three different thought patterns that all of us have experienced.

In Chart A, the low frequency line is a measure of a negative thought pattern, while the high frequency line is a measurement of a positive thought pattern. The medium frequency wave represents a thought pattern that is somewhere in between the two. The height of each line is the same, which indicates an equal amplitude behind each thought.

Chart B shows two lines of the same frequency but of different amplitudes. The higher amplitude may reflect the involvement of more emotion; for example, more love in the positive or more anger in the negative.

A Sports Scenario

Let's apply a sports analogy to the information in Charts A and B. Imagine playing a team-sports game with equal scores on the board. You are playing a steady game and feeling good about your performance, so the frequency of your thought pattern is reasonably quick, because it is positive. When somebody on your team does something that inspires you, you feel even better. The vibration of your thought pattern quickens (the waves grow closer together) because you've become more confident. This increase in your thought vibration, in turn, creates more positive outcomes (thoughts create outcomes). You may even notice that the whole team is more positive as well. Then you make a spectacular play, scoring a totally unexpected goal for the team. Your frequency increases and your excitement (emotion) creates a sharp rise in the amplitude of your thoughts, which hit a rare high. As a result, you get a large release of adrenalin and you start playing above your own expectations, because your new self-belief is powerful (amplitude) and very positive (frequency). Your performance lifts the whole team and now everybody has a high-frequency thought pattern with high amplitude created by the excitement. Your team is on a roll and, providing you can all hold that enthusiasm, you will play above your normal standards and are more likely to win.

The scenario above highlights another universal principle: the law of opposite polarities. Your team's high creates a potential low for your opponents. They will struggle as a lower vibration creeps into their thought patterns. They may have been fairly positive about their ability to win, but when confronted with the lower vibration energy of doubt, they are also likely to feel emotionally flat and realize they need to "lift their game" to get back on top. But, your team is on a high, playing with such confidence, so they are going to have to raise their standard above yours to get to a level at which they can compete. Let's assume that the talent of the players on both sides is even. Your opposing team not only has to deal with a side playing above its normal level, but they also have to contend with the negative energy created by the opposite polarity of your positive energy. Having to rise above their low-vibrating energy with accompanying low amplitude is hard—but not nearly as difficult as a low-vibrating energy that has a high amplitude. The strength of amplitude applies whether the accompanying vibration is positive or negative. Whereas excitement and enthusiasm create the high amplitude of positive energy, an overwhelming feeling of possible defeat may trigger a powerful amplitude accompanying a negative vibration.

The difference in the vibrations and amplitudes between the winning and losing sides may be easy enough to understand.

All those actions and outcomes started with the thoughts of the individual players, which combined with similar thoughts of their team members (like attracts like); these thoughts accumulate to create a much more powerful energy. This unseen energy is detected by other like-minded players; it combines with individual thought patterns and is amplified. The stronger thought pattern and positive emotions radiate outward and cycles of compatible energies interact with each other, creating momentum. The team members feel as though they are "on a roll," because their positive actions are being supported by a very positive energy, which they are creating, attracting, and receiving through the "air waves" (the ether). The same system is being played out with the losing side, only the accumulating thought-energy is negative.

You may have noticed in your own sporting experiences that everything seems to go in your favour and your moves and actions just seem to work when you are feeling positive and very confident. The opposite happens when you have self-doubt and feel negative. You put the same effort in, in both scenarios, so it is not a lack of striving that makes the difference, nor does your skill level. The difference is more likely psychological—a negative state of mind—which is very hard to shift in the midst of being affected by it. It is well known that, at the elite level of sports, the power and discipline of the mind often separates the very best from the rest of the pack. Such athletes have the ability to stay highly positive and focused even when things aren't going their way.

In 2017, Roger Federer was the number one tennis player in the world and had won eighteen grand slams, which is a record for males. He could keep his cool and stay focused while under extreme pressure. He certainly had the talent, but he stayed calm and focused most of the time and showed very little emotion whether he was winning or losing. This kind of control of the mind reduces amplitude to virtually nil. He can hold positive energy without allowing emotions to create imbalance in his thinking, which allows him to concentrate. Federer offers a great role model for keeping a balanced mind. He is a true sportsman.

Some top athletes use emotion to ignite the fire in their bellies so that they can perform at their best. They get angry and shout, and this behaviour is tolerated in the name of entertainment. They create a high amplitude, which gets their adrenalin running, and they perform at their best. To a certain extent, this is seen as positive by many people who are usually most interested in winners and great entertainment—but such bad behaviour does not belong in the spiritual world because it lowers a person's vibration. One of the sad things about the anger-based energy generated in order to win is that children watch their idols acting like this and accept the behaviour as the norm, and may even imitate it. John McEnroe was a world number one tennis player during the 1980s. He was one of the first to introduce bad behaviour into the elite tennis world. He was branded as "the brat" by the media for a long time. However, he prevailed and many people put up with his on-court antics because of his talent. He was eventually inducted into the International Tennis Hall of Fame regardless of his bad behaviour. Now the international tennis circuit has many ill-tempered players, and it may be frowned upon but it is tolerated.

The world generally accepts this kind of behaviour in sports and many other endeavours. Level-headed athletes are often overshadowed by highly emotionally charged players who are spiritually out of balance. Winning is everything and they aim to win at all costs. We can see this same scenario playing out in all walks of life. Humankind has generally succumbed to the pleasures of the ego, which prefers high amplitudes over the discipline and rewards that come with balance and harmony. This negative path creates a very long road to attaining divinity.

THE PATH OF LEAST RESISTANCE

As we have discussed, energy is always moving and if it did not move then it would not exist. It is also moving towards the positive or the negative but only in one direction in any given moment. Another important characteristic of energy is that it naturally follows the path of least resistance. Let's consider electricity as an example. Electricity travels through certain materials better than others. Materials that it most easily flows through are called conductors and materials that resist this flow are called insulators. The power-line wires that carry electricity from point A to point B are held in place by poles. These poles usually have a cross arm, on the end of which are the insulators that attach to the power line. The insulators prevent the electricity from conducting down the poles and into the ground or perhaps electrocuting someone who touched the pole. The power lines are composed of conductive material, providing a medium through which the electricity can easily travel. In effect, the electricity is following the path of least resistance and it is *controlled* by the materials used. Conductive materials provide the least resistance, while insulators provide the most resistance. Plastic and rubber materials provide good resistance, while copper wire is one of the best conductors. This is why the extension leads that we use around the house are covered with PVC or a similar material.

Let's explore this a little further. Are some materials better conductors than others? Copper, aluminum, and silver are very good conductors. If these metals were kept separate but hooked up to provide a system that allowed electricity to travel down any or all of the three at the same time, the electricity would flow down the silver conductor. It would bypass the other two metals because they are more resistant than silver. If we removed the silver wire from the experiment, then the electricity would flow along the copper wire because copper is a greater conductor than aluminum. It would obviously flow down the aluminum if the other two materials were not present. This is an example of how energy always chooses the path of least resistance. Doing so makes sense, because it requires the least amount of energy. It is natural to conserve energy and not natural to waste it.

We, too, are naturally attracted to the easiest path, because it requires the least effort. Humans will take the easier path, even if it is to their detriment. It is so easy to forego self-discipline, because self-discipline requires greater mind power (which involves more energy) than just letting things go. Almost all humans have bad habits that we would rather not have, but to change them requires effort, which takes energy. The natural law draws us towards not changing and so resistance sets in. People get stuck in old habits and they stay there until they make a conscious choice to change. Many people don't engage the energy necessary for change, and so their negative habits slowly but surely become compulsions or addictions. Discipline requires effort, and a lack of discipline requires very little, if no energy at all. All change requires the initiative to rise above the law that energy will always follow the path of least resistance. Overcoming this law is one of our greatest challenges; however, we must conquer it if we are to live the divinity of the highest levels of consciousness.

The human race has a history of resisting change and, therefore, it keeps repeating its old, negative patterns. One such pattern sees us repeatedly at the brink of self-annihilation—but, so far, we have escaped that outcome. The pattern of least resistance keeps playing out, because the vast majority of people don't make the effort to create change, which must start with their own lives. People generally want to blame other people, governments, institutions, the system, bad luck, fate, and so on, for what happens in their world. Blaming anything or anyone outside yourself helps move the cause away from yourself. This may create temporary relief from your own emotional pain, but deflecting the blame allows you to stay in denial of the fact that you created it on some level (often subconsciously). Blaming others keeps you on the path of least resistance, because you don't have to deal with your problem if someone or something else is the cause.

Most people tend to blame others because they don't know any different. There are some who do know what to do, but they avoid facing the responsibility that comes with owning their own creations—this is also the path of least resistance, because it doesn't require any energy to maintain the status quo. However, there are a few people who do take responsibility and put effort into changing, which doesn't come easy and can often be stressful. Under any kind of stress, our brain goes into survival mode, activating our primitive brain, which resists change. (There will be more on this in Chapter 5.) It is not hard to see why the humans are so slow at shifting their consciousness to a higher level. We prefer our natural tendency to maintain the path of least resistance.

Some people may feel discouraged by the last paragraph and wonder whether they will ever have the strength and willpower to reach their full potential. This information is a bit like the statement, "know thy enemy." It's intended to provide people with the knowledge about what they're dealing with when they feel that resistance. People are much less likely to be dragged under if they know what's happening. Information arms us with the awareness to recognize something when it arises. Many people fall over because they don't know how to handle the hurdles of life. We all can rise above resistance to become the masters of our own destiny. There is middle ground between giving in to the temptation to follow the path of least resistance and determining to strive ahead at all costs. This middle ground is found in the law of balance. The path of least resistance also has a huge effect on the choices we make about evolving our consciousness. Both of these laws will be revisited later in this chapter.

TO DO OR NOT TO DO

Energy is always moving. It is never dormant. When we choose *to do* something, we are activating energy. Providing that our choice is positive, the energy we use moves us towards the positive. If we choose *not to do* anything, then we are not using energy, which is similar to dormancy. A dormant state directs the flow of energy towards the negative, so from this perspective, in inaction we move backwards. When the choice *not to do* represents the path of least resistance, growth is hindered. In other words, we slowly but surely move towards the negative when we are being complacent or inactive. The term "fence sitter" implies that a person is reluctant to or not interested enough to have an opinion, get involved, or take action. But their lack of involvement means that a part of their energy is moving towards the negative. In the end, a person can't be a fence sitter forever, because the accumulating negative energy will become very obvious. They will eventually want to become a doer, becoming active and getting involved.

Choosing *to do nothing* is almost the same as *not doing* anything, but the former is a conscious choice, while the latter is the result of a lack of conscious involvement. Both create an environment that causes our energy to move towards the negative.

One of the characteristics that separate humans from animals is that we have free will and choice. Our free will allows us to do anything we want, although a high degree of responsibility comes with free will. If we want to spiritually evolve, then we have to exercise the choice to do so. In many instances, we don't do anything about our spiritual growth, not because we've chosen to do nothing but because we have not made a choice at all. However, there are consequences for inaction. If we don't make a decision to spiritually grow, then we aren't moving towards the positive. By default, we must be moving towards the negative. Considering this fact, our spiritual growth is best served by having a never-ending commitment. Spiritual life could be described as "a never-ending story."

If we take these two choices into account in light of the principle that energy is moving towards either the positive or the negative and is never stationary, it becomes apparent that we are always making choices that either enhance our spiritual journey or hinder it. We may make choices that lower our vibration, which will take us backwards on our spiritual journey. Some people are not even aware of the need to consciously evolve, and such lack of awareness is regressive on a spiritual journey.

THE LAW OF ATTRACTION

This universal law states that *like attracts like* and *opposites repel each other*. It is hugely influential over the human race. Humans are generally attracted to like-minded people. Groups of people are drawn together because of their similar interests. We normally prefer to mix with people who think the same way we do, and the more we have in common, the likelier we are to build strong friendships. This happens on all levels. For example, people who uphold the law tend to come together, while criminals are attracted to each other. People of strong spiritual beliefs mix, while people who oppose spirituality tend to mingle. People with strong similar political persuasions network together, to name but a few examples.

Let's consider how this energy of attraction operates.

Energy is naturally cyclical—it will always return to the point at which it was created. Our mind continuously generates either positive or negative energies, but never at the same time. Every thought that you produce is either positive or negative. Thought patterns are formed from individual thoughts. You have the ability to control what you think on the conscious level. But you are not consciously in control of the thoughts that your subconscious mind generates in any given moment. *Your subconscious mind generates a far greater percentage of your total thoughts than your conscious mind does.*

It is easy enough to recognize what we consciously think by applying self-observation. Almost everyone regularly reflects on their thoughts. We can also control what we are thinking and make choices about what we want to think about. But what about our subconscious thoughts? Since most of our thoughts are happening at a subconscious level, it's advantageous to have some tools to help us recognize what thoughts we are generating from there.

Energy Resonance

There is another characteristic of energy that is closely aligned with the law of attraction and that affects other planes of consciousness. It has to do with how other, specific levels resonate to a particular vibration. When we have thoughts, not only do we generate energy that affects the earth plane, but the vibration of thought patterns travels out and reverberates throughout the universe. This is like an echo that transmits through the different dimensions, and the specific vibration of this energy triggers a response with all resonant vibrations. Using an analogy with sound helps make this concept clear. If you strike middle C on a piano, then the C that is one octave above will also vibrate in response. In other words, it will resonate to middle C. This is a very simplistic example, but hopefully it helps elucidate the concept. The energy of thoughts creates a response, and because of the cyclical nature of energy, the effect of this response will return to its origin, which is the original thoughts. This explanation is reinforced in the next section: cause and effect.

Cause and Effect

When we create a vibration with our thoughts, we are triggering other similar energies, not only on the earth plane, but in all other dimensions as well. These triggered vibrations send back more of the same energy, and so the energy associated with our thoughts gets amplified. In this way, our intentions are supported by the universe. In other words, we trigger universal energy with our thoughts and intentions and when that energy returns, its power is stronger than the power of our original thoughts. There are two spiritual teachings that relate to this process. The first is that *we reap what we sow*, meaning that what we create will come back for us to experience. If we do bad things, then bad things will happen to us. Likewise, if we do good things, then good things will happen to us. (This is governed by the universal principle that energy naturally moves in cycles.) The second is that *what we sow will come back to us tenfold*, meaning that the universe will respond with a lot more energy than we initially created. (This is partly governed by the universal principles of energy resonance and the law of attraction.) This second teaching also highlights the fact that several universal principles can be involved in any given situation.

Thought, Word, and Deed

Anything we create goes through a three-stage process. We start with an original thought or idea. If we don't think any more about it, then it's normally quickly forgotten and nothing more happens. We activate the second stage by thinking more about the subject—which may include mulling it over in our mind and involving our imagination. We may write the idea down or make a sketch or plan. This gives the original thought more power because we are accruing similar thoughts. The third stage begins when we manifest the original thought by acting on it. Thus, we have the three-stage process of thought, word, and deed. The first stage is the "cause" and the last stage is the "effect."

Cause and Effect in the Subconscious

Seeing the creative process in something tangible, experienced through our five senses, and that has a recognizable effect on a conscious level is easy. However, generally we are not aware of what we create on a subconscious level. If we are not conscious of what we are creating, then it's unlikely we'll know what cause we're generating either. To know what we're creating, all we can do is turn to the effect to find the answer. If we can discern it with one of our five senses, then we are more likely to recognize what we have created. How do we recognize the thoughts that don't manifest in a tangible way? Because energy always cycles, we can trust that thoughts will always come back to us in one form or another. We need to monitor what comes to us to see what we are initially creating.

Thoughts are a powerful form of energy, and energy moves in cycles. Every thought has a vibration and positive thoughts have a higher vibration than negative thoughts do. A thought travels out from our mind and is picked up by the people around us (similarly to how an antenna picks up a radio signal).

Energy and the Creative Process | 71

This information is processed through their mind/brain systems, and they will respond according to their perceptions, which are regulated by their belief systems. People respond in different ways, according to their beliefs. Their responses initially create thoughts. Their thoughts will either create a verbal or physical response, and so on, or simply a thought-energy that our mind receives via its own antenna. This incoming thought-energy may trigger a feeling, which may or may not trigger an emotion, but we probably won't know why, how, or where it came from. Even though such a response is incredibly subtle, it still has effect, even if it is immeasurable.

Here is a possible scenario. You express an opinion in a group conversation. Everybody in the group processes that information according to their personal belief systems and they respond accordingly. There are several different opinions on the subject at hand so what you hear (the energy coming back to you) is the response to your original thoughts, which have now been filtered by their beliefs. Some people respond positively while others react negatively. Remember that you can only control and be responsible for your thoughts, not theirs. What comes back to you is not a true reflection of what you sent out, because it has been filtered by others' thought processes. If the energy coming back to you is not exactly the same as what you sent out, how do you interpret and learn from the returning energy? You know that their different responses are a result of their conscious and subconscious belief systems. This also means that how you respond to their responses also comes from both your conscious and subconscious beliefs.

What are the responsibilities of all involved? Everyone is responsible for two main aspects of the process. Firstly, we are all responsible for our thoughts, words, and actions. Secondly, and more challengingly, we are responsible for how we receive and react to the thoughts, words, and actions or reactions of others. We are not responsible for how they receive the information, nor are they responsible for how we receive their reaction. For example, we may say or do something that upsets somebody. Their reaction may alert us to their feelings, but we are not responsible for those feelings. We are only responsible for what we said or did. We may need to ask ourselves the motive for what we said. They might feel angry and direct that anger at us. Many people react this way because they don't want to own, or are not aware enough to realize, that they create their own anger, so they blame whatever triggered it. Nobody can trigger anger if there is no anger to trigger. This anger is normally hidden in the subconscious. The best thing to do is note that what is coming back to you is not always a true reflection of your original thoughts.

What happens next is critical to whether you learn from the interaction. You will always have an immediate response to any incoming information in the form of a thought, feeling, or emotion. This initial response is uncontrolled because it happens before your mind has had time to get involved. These responses are the result of your brain processing the information against your long-term memory data system. It will trigger a thought, feeling, or emotion so quickly that you probably won't be aware of it unless you're looking for it. This initial response is your clue to your personal truth, because it is purely a response using the data held in your long-term memory. Your second response is a controlled response of the mind and it kicks in almost immediately, making many first responses easy to ignore. Once your mind gets to work, you will start to use your conscious mind and brain processes to produce a response that you can control.

If your initial, subconscious response and your second, conscious response are the same, then both thought patterns are in sync. If your delayed reaction is different than the initial response, then what you really believe and what you want to (or should) believe are out of sync. A common phrase used to describe this initial response is "a knee-jerk reaction," and people sometimes get embarrassed about what they have said or done. Another related expression is "think before you speak." People sometimes feel embarrassed about what they say during an initial response and try to correct or justify it: They spoke without thinking. If they had waited until their mind cut in, they could have used reason and control. However, the first reaction is the result of the brain processing its subconscious long-term memory data, without the influence of the mind. This is their personal truth. It could be said that is what they really think.

Awareness of the two stages of response to what others say and do provides the data needed to operate your own self-monitoring system. An accurate system will enable you to understand what you hold in your conscious and subconscious belief systems. Let's presume that somebody says something negative and even hurtful and you hear it. It may or may not be true or even directed at you, but that does not matter. It does not even matter whether the words are positive or negative. Your response to that incoming or returning energy is what really matters. If incoming data has a negative effect on you, then you have a negative belief that has been triggered. This belief may be on a conscious or subconscious level or even both. If you have a negative response, then you have negative data in your long-term memory. It has to be there somewhere because it is impossible to trigger something that is not there. As we climb to the higher levels of self-awareness, we all become aware of our most painful and hidden negatives along with our deepest, darkest secrets. You will learn so much about yourself if you observe your first and second responses with an opened and non-judgemental mind.

EXERCISE 4: IDENTIFYING THOUGHTS AND FEELINGS

Practise becoming aware of your thoughts and feelings:

1. The next time you are talking with someone, see if you can discern your initial response and the second one, which comes almost immediately after the first.
2. Sometimes there may be a longer delay between the responses. Remember that the initial response is often so quick that unless you are focused you may miss it.
3. If there is no change in your thoughts and feelings during both stages, then it may be that you have no issue or that both your conscious and subconscious are in sync.

Here is an example of the two stages being different: A friend accuses you of being angry about something they said. Your initial reaction is a feeling of anger, but you control the anger (second response), present yourself as calm, and then deny that you feel angry. There is a more extreme example of this scenario. You can become so expert at denying the anger that you actually get to the point where you can't feel the initial anger and so believe that you are really not angry. This denial is a form of suppression, with those feelings of anger buried so deep into your subconscious that you're no longer conscious of them. We all master suppressing many unwanted emotions during our childhood, but the unwanted feelings still exist. They become hidden in our subconscious and covertly generate angry thoughts that we're not even aware of. Yet, we emit these thoughts and they have an effect on everybody and everything around us. They also create negative energy that attacks the cells in our body, and much of our ill health starts with these covert thought patterns.

The more you practise becoming aware of the first stage response, the likelier you will be able to recognize the fleeting, split-second associated feelings or emotions.

OPPOSITE POLARITIES

Energy has opposite polarities, also known as positive and negative. The charts earlier in this chapter illustrated that one cannot exist without the other and their amplitude will also be the exact opposite. In other words, the more positive something is, the more negative its opposite potential will be as well. You may notice that when you come down off a high, there's often a low. Some people talk about their experiences on drugs as a "real high" and describe the effects of coming off drugs as "a real downer." The highs and lows are direct opposites of each other. If someone is a little bit happy, then there exists the potential of experiencing its opposite, a little bit unhappy. If someone is very happy, then they create the potential of experiencing its opposite, very unhappy. The more extreme the emotion is, the more extreme its opposite will be.

Young people usually want to experience the excitement of life and have a great time while doing so. However, excitement takes up energy, and no one can use the energy involved in experiencing excitement forever. At some point, we have to stop, and this is often followed by a period of feeling flat or even very low. Many older people are content to enjoy life without all the excitement. The younger generations probably think that this is boring because they want the good feelings that come with being positively charged. However, after having lived an exciting lifestyle, older people often choose a quieter existence because they prefer a steady, balanced life rather than one filled with highs and lows. If you want to live an exciting life then you are likely to choose the highs and deal with their opposite lows as they come along. Highs are usually great fun, but the lows may leave you feeling way out of balance. Some people get so far out of balance that they don't feel life is worth living. When a person becomes that negative, it is a very hard road back to a balanced, harmonious, bearable life.

Older people who still have their faculties are generally a lot wiser than younger generations give them credit for. They have lived a lot, and wisdom can only be gained by experience. We can study and gain knowledge, but wisdom comes from applying that knowledge to life. Those with very high academic qualifications have gained much knowledge, but knowledge by itself is just information that we retain in our long-term memory. How we use and apply that information to life is what separates the wise from the not so wise. Not all people need to grow old to become wise. Some show real wisdom at an early age. However, younger people who show wisdom will likely be much wiser as they live life, apply their knowledge, and learn from their experiences. We never stop experiencing, so we always have the opportunity to learn and to become wiser.

The earth's opposite polarities are the North and South Poles. The North Pole is a positive energy and the South Pole is negative. As you now know, for energy to exist it must be moving, either moving towards the positive or the negative. We need these opposites to be able to experience life on earth. They create reference points through which we can relate to life. Everything that we do has either a positive or negative aspect to it. Here is a list of some opposites that we are all familiar with:

Positive	Negative
Love	Fear
Night	Day
Sad	Happy
Male	Female
Left	Right
Up	Down
Good	Bad
Wrong	Right

These opposites create clear reference points that make things easily recognizable as one or the other. One side is not better than the other—they are only opposites.

Law of Balance

The law of balance is the greatest of all the universal laws. Balance and harmony go together. Balance creates harmony and harmony creates balance. Balance affects all other universal laws, and when all universal laws are in balance with each other, there will be harmony within the universe. When our lives are in balance, we experience harmony. The more we're out of balance, the more disharmony we experience. It requires more energy to stay out of balance than it does to stay in balance. The further out of balance we become, the more energy it takes to stay there. Staying really positive or really negative both require a lot of energy. For example, a weekend full of endless fun and laughter will normally leave us feeling very tired on Monday. If we have had a weekend full of stress, then it may be hard to get out of bed on Monday, too. If we are feeling really positive and we don't maintain the energy to hold that state, then we will slide backwards until we reach a state of balance. We need to become aware of what this state of balance feels like, become familiar with it, and focus on maintaining it. If we don't, then we will probably keep sliding down towards the negative.

Sliding from the positive to the negative is the norm for most people, but it may not be conscious. Many people are not aware of how the principle of opposites functions. Some people slide backwards simply because they are too lazy to move forwards, towards the positive. Any slide towards the negative will eventually end because the further we get out of balance the stronger the negative charge becomes. This charge will eventually become so strong that it will be unbearable.

The desperation to get out of this state becomes the motivational factor to make us seek positivity or balance. We need to understand that the further we slide into negative territory, the harder the road back becomes. Some people spend many years lifting themselves out of their negative situation. However, the positive side of this is that the hardest lessons in life are normally what we gain the most awareness from.

Aligning Ourselves with the Universal Laws

When we are in balance with any universal law, we are also in balance with the highest level of truth possible. The two charts earlier in this chapter show us that perfect balance is represented by a flat line. No high and low amplitudes are experienced at this level and no obvious vibration can be seen either. This also means that no emotion or positive energy shows at all, and this might seem to be a contradiction in terms of how we need to live. If this flat line represents perfect balance and harmony, then how does a vibration created by love and amplitude created by emotion have an effect? Here is the explanation.

When we reach enlightenment, every aspect of our energy field will be vibrating in harmony with the vibrations created by the highest truths. Right now, we have some personal truths that are of a higher consciousness than others. We cannot be sure which ones are and which ones are not. The ones that aren't will show up at some stage. What happens if we concentrate on purifying our mind and increasing the power of our love? We effectively increase the overall vibration of our energy field. The areas of our life that are in balance with the highest truths cannot vibrate higher because they are already vibrating as high as they can. They will be of a very high vibration with little or no amplitude and, therefore, very little effort is required to maintain them. This is reflected in the flat line of balance in the energy charts. (Amplitude requires effort.) Areas of our life that are out of balance will start to heal as we purify our mind. The aim is to bring these areas into balance with the highest truths. As these areas come into balance their vibration increases and they have an effect on the overall energy field. As more aspects of our energy field come into alignment with higher truths, we will have less conflict and resistance to change, and so exert less in creating powerful love. Before we reach enlightenment, we can expect to have some aspects of our life creating negative amplitude. The amplitude created by the love from our heart will help balance that out until higher consciousness is reached. Keep in mind that these changes start by purifying our thoughts. We need healthy thoughts, because love alone is not enough to create balance and harmony.

It was mentioned before that we could also call universal laws, universal principles. The word "law" fits in with an old paradigm, because it implies that something is either right or wrong. That fits perfectly into a consciousness based on opposite polarities. However, human consciousness is moving towards a new paradigm that includes levels of truth. This means that laws give away to principles in the same way as right and wrong gives away to levels of truth.

Omni-energy and the Third Dimension
We are living on the earth plane and, therefore, we obviously have not evolved back to the Oneness where we started out many lifetimes ago. The Oneness energy is "omni-energy," which is the same as that of its Creator—the "first cause." Omni-energy is all-encompassing and experiences all potentials, everything at once—the highs and lows of energy; the past, present, and future; the good and bad; the here and there; the up and down—because there is no beginning nor

end and no separation. It does not separate its experiences of everything because it is everything and that is why it is called Omni. This means the high and low amplitudes, along with the high and low vibrations, are inseparable. There is no definable vibration or amplitude. The third dimension allows for the experience of separation and individuality, which is set up to make the human experience possible. God experiences life through us. We were created as individual spirits who have free will and choice to experience whatever we create on the earth plane. How can we be judged for doing exactly what we were created to do? We won't be punished for making negative spiritual choices from a low level of consciousness such as ignorance. God does not punish us; we punish ourselves by creating negative karma. Although karma is not actually a punishment, because it is the result of energy in its natural cycle.

Here is a summary of how the characteristics of our spiritual awareness are reflected in the two charts on vibration:

- The most negative choices and experiences of the human experience slow our vibrations down.
- The most positive choices and experiences increase our vibrations to prepare us for the experience of higher planes of consciousness.
- Strong emotions of love and fear create high amplitude.
- Finding balance between the opposite polarities brings us closer to living in balance with the universal principles.
- Balance creates inner peace and harmony. This is reflected by the wave motion of its vibration being almost a flat line.
- Inner peace and harmony are above the need for the amplitude created by high positive emotion in order to enjoy life.

Personal Versus the Universal State of Balance

Many people have been in a negative state for so long that they think it is normal and may feel quite balanced. They have only found a personal state of balance that creates the least resistance, which is the easiest way for them to live. The balance they have found is the middle ground between their more positive state and their more negative state. This middle ground is less stressful than their more extreme negative territory and so it feels good. If someone were to ask them how they feel, they would probably say they feel good, even if they were in a state of mild depression. This state of balance is not the same as being in balance with the relevant universal law. It is like moving the line of balance downwards into negative territory and then believing that state is true balance because it feels comfortable. This same situation applies to those who have created a very positive personal balance. This higher state could be seen as a false security because, thinking they have already found it, they are not likely to seek higher truths that will lead them into true balance.

The only way to really know if we are in balance with a relevant universal law is by being tested. Our concepts need a reality check and we test them by observing ourselves honestly. The measure is, if we have total inner peace, calmness, and harmony when an issue arises, then we have total balance—providing we have accompanying compassion and understanding. No emotional charge will be involved. This is different than being disinterested and unfeeling, lacking any sign of emotion. Be vigilant and gentle with yourself and do not judge yourself for what you uncover. You need to feel happy about uncovering any negative states. Remember that you will only be able to grow to the next level after you have recognized and dealt with issues of the level you are on. Not being prepared to uncover a negative or an overcharged positive has the same effect as being in a state of denial.

People who feel balanced when they're actually in really negative territory need to make a real effort to become positive before they can come back into true balance. But how do we find balance if we are so far out of balance? If a very negative person wants to find balance in their life, the natural suggestion is that they should aim for the middle energy (or flat line) of balance. This may be the ideal, but it requires great amounts of energy and commitment. The further away from the line of balance we move, the more energy is required to maintain our status quo. A huge effort is required to go from extreme negativity into extreme positive territory to counteract and balance out the energy. The most common experience is that people can't hold that positive energy for very long and they fall back into the negative state once again. That is okay, because some of the positive energy goes with them when they go back into the negative state, thus they don't fall back as far as they were before the positive experience. It is rare to move from a very negative state into a state of balance. Nearly everyone seesaws between the opposite polarities but, when the goal is to achieve balance, the amplitude diminishes each time they swing. Slowly but surely the heights and depths of amplitude reduce and so does the correlated effort required. Eventually, holding a more balanced state becomes easy.

Another analogy for this seesawing between the positive and negative is that of a swinging pendulum. If you swing a pendulum and let it go until it stops, each time it swings, the distance of the arc gets smaller until it stops in the middle. The highest point of the swing relates to the strongest amplitude. The momentum dies down, and then the pendulum stops. When there is no swing between the positive and negative poles, we might think that we have achieved perfect harmony. The opposite poles have actually lost their influence on the pendulum and this creates a form of balance. If that balance is

Energy and the Creative Process | 83

not aligned with the highest truth, then we can expect that an imbalance will eventually show up.

We may have no charge on a subject because we simply don't care enough to create one. We could be totally indifferent because the issue doesn't affect us personally. Second, someone who was extremely out of balance and is now experiencing comparatively much less negativity often feels happy with the new level of balance they have found. It feels great and so they enjoy that level rather than committing more effort to searching for the ultimate state. The closer they move towards balance, the less the effort required to hold that state. It takes a much bigger issue to trigger any emotional response. There is no right or wrong, and they will probably be content until a reality check tests them once again.

Here's a scenario that illustrates the aspects of the law of balance explored above: A great debate about the need to build a new sporting complex rages in your community. It is a very big issue and the arguments for and against are emotionally charged. There is almost no balance in the arguments because of the strong points of view. The law of opposing polarities is playing out. Conflicting forces, with their emotionally charged points of view, add amplitude to the debate. Both sides believe they are right and so the other must be wrong. Thus, no middle ground is reached. Both sides are so blinded by their own bias on the subject that they are beyond the point of being able to see the other side's point of view. It is unlikely that any resolution will be reached in such a situation.

Naming the causes of climate change is creating a similar divide worldwide. Highly charged, opposing arguments are being debated across the globe, from the top levels of science to governments and societies to the local level of friends and families. If the survival of humanity is threatened by what happens to our climate, then we need to slow or stop the climate from changing. Carbon emissions from the industrialized world is a primary cause, and many industries' profits could be severely reduced if we are to significantly cut carbon emissions quickly. However, time may be running out. Evidence about the severity of the problem produced by some science is hotly counteracted by those who challenge that data. Many self-invested interests are sabotaging the chance to have a balanced debate, thus to create a balanced outcome. The amplitude of the imbalance is extreme and efforts to locate middle ground (balance) are being sabotaged. Eventually, there will be a reality check, and hopefully not too late to benefit humanity.

People from all parts of the globe are above this type of behaviour. For example, a highly evolved person brings balance into the debate because they are able to see both sides and the middle ground. Some may see such people as weak or indifferent because their opinions are not forceful, but in fact they are very wise. A highly evolved person would not condone or condemn either side but would show great compassion for both sides.

The middle ground achieved from wisdom is much more balanced than anything achieved through compromises made purely for the sake of a resolution. Compromise may create an acceptable outcome for all parties involved, but if it is not true balance, then imbalances will show up as a project progresses. The universe will expose any imbalance for what it is, because anything less than the highest truth creates an imbalance. Imbalances will always appear as faults or disharmony. We can see these laws playing out in humanity. There are endless committees and organizations around the world endeavouring to seek the middle ground of compromise and peace. Nearly all of them fail to find permanent solutions because the basic philosophies that underpin human consciousness are faulty and, therefore, out of balance with universal truths.

To summarize, let's consider how we know when we've found perfect balance in an area of our life. It is when an issue arises and we have no emotional charge around it. We still have feelings, but they will be of calmness and inner peace, accompanied by compassion and interest. Then we will know that our total belief system (comprising the conscious and subconscious) is in balance with that particular universal truth. When we experience this level of consciousness, we will know a part of our divinity.

5

The Brain

The control centre of the physical being.

THE HUMAN brain is an incredible organ with amazing abilities that have the capacity to make us feel happy or unhappy, lucky or unlucky, live a successful life, or even destroy us. It can send positive or negative signals to other parts of our body and thus control their status. The effect can keep them in homeostasis (balance) or in a state of decay and chaos. That ability is very powerful. Our brain can also affect our spiritual climb to higher consciousness because some of its functions can either enhance or seriously hinder our efforts, if we allow it. To create the life we want, we need to respect and understand our brain, learn to control it, and feed it the right information.

Over many thousands, possibly millions, of years, the human brain has evolved through three stages of development. The third stage of development has given us the ability to be so creative and to speed up our spiritual evolution. It has increased our ability to search, research, and understand our self physically, psychologically, and spiritually. This has helped us discern the higher purpose of our existence and our relationship with the Creator. The three stages are known as the first, second, and third brains. Regarding their relevance to the evolution of our consciousness, all three stages are integrated and function as one brain. The following information is intended to be a very basic presentation in order to present functions of a very complex organ relevant to our conversation.

The First Brain

Also known as the reptilian brain, the first brain is an organ of "primitive humans" and it functions for survival:

- It controls our basic bodily functions, such as breathing, heart rate, and digestion.
- It is driven by instincts, such as to eat, drink, and reproduce.
- It controls balance and coordination.

The Second Brain

The second brain is the emotional centre:

- It is the seat of short-term memory.
- It registers rewards and punishment.
- It also controls expression and emotion.
- It, along with its slave (the reptilian brain), appears to control instinctive responses to fear and threat, such as the fight-or-flight modes, which are involuntary behaviour.

The Third Brain

The third brain controls conscious thought and voluntary movement:

- Abstract thinking occurs here.
- It is the seat of long-term memory.
- It is the most adept at learning new ways of adapting and coping.
- It seems to be responsible for voluntary behaviour and thinking, speaking, and acting in socially accepted ways.

THE MIND AND THE BRAIN

Let's explore the interaction between our brain and the mind. I often refer to the universal mind as "our mind" to give it a more personal perspective and because it is a localized part of the bigger mind. We use the mind to generate thoughts, which are a form of consciousness. Even though these thoughts are only one form of consciousness, they are still very powerful and have a huge effect on our life. The mind is dynamic and operates on both conscious and subconscious levels. Our mind interacts with our brain and, to a certain extent, their joint functions control the life we live. If we are going to evolve and take charge of our life, then it is paramount to understand how we can influence the functions of these two centres. We use our mind to control some of the functions of our brain. Our brain can also operate without directions or instructions from our mind. To operate from a much higher level of consciousness, we not only need to know how we can control our minds, we also need to recognize the things that hold us back.

It will be beneficial to understand:

- How and why we find it hard to let go of old beliefs that no longer serve us;
- How to transform the beliefs we no longer need;
- How our perceptions and attitudes are formed;
- Why we are naturally biased and the purpose of bias;

- Why and how our negative emotions and reactions get triggered; and
- Why we judge others and why is it so natural to do so.

The answers to these questions are woven through this chapter and those to come.

Short-Term Memory

Short-term memory (STM) is housed in the second brain. All incoming data (information) is initially held in our short-term memory. Much of the information that makes its way into our STM comes from what we experience via our five senses: touch, smell, sight, hearing, and taste. Our mind can get involved at this stage and we can analyze and make choices about this data. For example, it will ask questions like, what does this information mean to me? Do I like it or not? Is it useful or not? Do I want to keep it or not? The information is only held in our STM for a short while, thus its name. If the information is not required, then we tend to forget it and erase it from our STM reasonably quickly. There is no longer a recording of the experience or information. In other words, if we don't think that it is important enough to remember or if we don't make an effort to remember, then we will lose information. Our five senses are sending huge amounts of information to our STM all the time, particularly while we are awake. Most of this information is lost.

Long-Term Memory

Long-term memory (LTM) is housed in the third brain. Any information recorded in our long-term memory becomes permanent. Our ability to recall it may change or be limited; however, the recording remains, as does the potential to recall any of this information. Our perceptions and beliefs are closely related to the data held in our LTM.

When we are awake, we transfer information from our STM to our LTM mainly by repetition and emotion. An example of the repetition method is learning the twelve times table in school by repetition until it is committed to memory. The repetition registers the information in our LTM so that it is readily available and takes very little effort to recall. The armed forces do weapons drills and ambulance officers practise CPR drills. These drills are a specific form of repetition designed to imprint the procedure on the LTM, so that it becomes habitual and automatically carried out when required, particularly under stress.

Emotion is an incredibly powerful characteristic of human personalities. When used properly, it has a huge effect on our spiritual evolution. For embedding information in our LTM, it is also more powerful than repetition. Information will pass immediately from the STM to the LTM, if the associated emotion is powerful enough. The reason is because our brains prioritize survival (as in a first/second brain function, such as fight-or-flight). If our life is in danger, then we will do what we need to do to survive. The terror created in that moment will generate enough fear-based emotion to transfer the memory of the situation from our STM straight into our LTM. If the danger (or perceived danger) is triggered again by a similar event in the future, then we will automatically revert to survival mode, which will activate the same response that we recorded in our LTM during the original experience. Extreme fear becomes embedded in the memory so strongly that simply to recall the situation or to see a photo that reminds us of it will trigger a reaction, one that could be extremely powerful and that may seem to be an overreaction.

During an experience of danger, we might not have time to engage our mind and think about what to do. We just do what we need to do to survive. However, this can lead to a state of trauma, in which we compulsively repeat our initial response.

We act to survive and analyze later. If we don't survive, then we won't be around to analyze anything!

Another important function of the LTM relates to our ability to recall the immense amount of information stored there. We want to recall only information that we need at a given time. It would be very confusing if we inadvertently recalled irrelevant information, so we have the ability to only recall the relevant information. The process of recall is triggered by association. Only information *associated* with whatever we are experiencing or thinking about in a moment is recalled. This also means that what we experience and record in our STM will trigger associated information in our LTM and this can happen without our mind's involvement. (This understanding is very important when it comes to the roles, responsibilities, and effects that both our subconscious mind and LTM play in our spiritual evolution.)

People act out what they have trained themselves, or have been trained, to do. This includes any stored information that is the result of influences from other people. Once information lodges in the LTM it becomes accepted information. It does not matter whether that information is positive or negative, the truth or a lie, helpful or a hindrance. Once it is registered in our LTM, it is a source for our belief system and, therefore, also for our personal truth. From this understanding, it's apparent why many people are vulnerable to certain types of manipulation by those who are clever enough to openly or covertly feed misinformation into people's LTMs.

This survival function of the brain is very important because it also has an affect that can enhance or hinder our spiritual evolution. The point that needs to be emphasized is that LTM data is built upon initial experiences, which potentially become core beliefs, and a core belief is the most influential belief that we can have on a subject. It is like the operating system of a computer. An efficient computer depends on a good operating system to process information. It is the same with our brain. Faulty or incorrect core beliefs have a huge negative influence on how we perceive things, plus how our brain processes future associated incoming data. Likewise, positive core beliefs have a very positive influence.

Once a core belief is established in our LTM, it becomes permanent. Many of our core beliefs are downloaded into our LTM by the ages of four to seven, which is about the age when we start to develop our ability to reason. Information does not have to make sense to a young child. It is what it is, and experiences become their reality or truth. Much of what we fundamentally believe in is not of our own making. It was placed there under the influence of what our parents believed or the beliefs of other influential people in our life at that time. Many organizations, including some religions, know this and their programs for teaching start with and are targeted at young children. It is possible to greatly influence young children because of their inability to discriminate between good and bad information. As explained, once that information becomes lodged in their LTM, then it becomes their truth. This information may be a lie or even totally evil but that does not matter. It has the ability to override any incoming information that is in conflict with it.

Although the effects of core beliefs can be overridden, most people don't put in the conscious effort required to do so. All around the world, people are dying all because others are acting out their very negative core beliefs. Our core beliefs are either our greatest friend or our worst enemy, and they are having a huge effect on the direction we are heading in our life. Negative beliefs usually go completely undetected because they mostly operate at a subconscious level; therefore, many people don't understand why their lives are so difficult. Fortunately, there are tools available that can help us uncover these negative subconscious thought patterns. I share some with you later in this book. Here is an exercise to get you started.

EXERCISE 5: IDENTIFYING THOUGHT PATTERNS

The purpose of this exercise is for you to start becoming aware of the thought patterns that have recurring positive or negative effects on your life. Look for the common denominators and see if you can identify any associated core beliefs that are driving or having a major influence on these outcomes. At this stage, focus on recognizing the patterns, not solving problems. This is an ongoing exercise intended to increase your awareness of your deeper belief systems that have the most effect on your past, present, and future:

1. Think about the parts of your life that come easily to you and the parts that are difficult.
2. Make a short list of the key positive and negative parts of your life. The initial step of this exercise is to bring these areas into your awareness so that you can start to observe them and how they affect you. Memorize and get to know them.
3. Next, start focusing on a more obvious positive part of your life that just seems to happen without much effort. Maybe it is something that you are good at or that you particularly like doing. Things just seem to go your way. It may seem like luck; however, in this model luck does not exist because *you create everything in your life.*

This is an ongoing process as it can take a lot of self-observation to uncover the deeper hidden core beliefs that quite often have the biggest influences on our life. Some core beliefs are associated with small, specific issues, while others influence many parts of our life. Stay open to looking for common denominators that show up in different areas. Some of the deeper negative beliefs can be very covert so they may require a much greater effort to bring them to the surface where you can consciously deal with them.

It is important to see how these core beliefs work in the positive before you look at how they work in the negative. Please, do yourself a favour and accept that fact. It is easy to own our positives but often very difficult to own our negatives. If you are genuine about self-exploration then you really have to believe that understanding your core beliefs will work for you. You will be far more prepared to tackle the negative aspects if you have positive proof that the concept works.

Here are three examples that show how core beliefs can work.

First, let's consider Tom. Tom is financially successful in life. Tom grew up in a positive family environment, where he learnt from his parents that if you work hard and are a shrewd business operator, then you will be successful. Those two principles made their way into his LTM and became core beliefs, which created outcomes in his life. Those beliefs work in Tom's favour and covertly and openly, making it easy for Tom to achieve in business. In fact, the beliefs are so ingrained that he doesn't really know any different. Tom is financially successful in life as a by-product of the two principles that guide him: he works hard and is a shrewd business operator.

Next, let's look at Jill, also a financially successful business person. Jill grew up in a negative family who thought that the world owed them something. Her parents believed that they were victims of an unfair system and that they had nothing to look forward to in life. They wallowed in self-pity and felt powerless to do anything about it. Jill was motivated—desperately and with determination—not to end up like her family, and she didn't take on their beliefs. Success came to Jill because of her inner drive, and every time she achieved something, it confirmed to her that she could and would be successful. Jill is not consciously aware of the driving force behind her success, but a subconscious core belief that she will take a different approach than her family automatically creates outcomes that help make her successful. The positive results reinforce her belief and so the belief grows stronger.

Jill's brother James grew up in the same negative family, but James took on a different core belief. James believed that his family really were victims, that life was going to be hard, and that there was no hope of ever being wealthy. As he grew up, he forgot about this core belief because he was a successful student who studied hard. He left the negativity of his parents behind as he developed a life of his own. He believed that life would be difficult but he believed that he could be successful if he worked hard. He then developed the belief that he could possibly be wealthy too, but he never saw his wealth accrue. Part of the original core belief was that there was no hope of ever being wealthy. Where there is *no hope*, the belief generates outcomes reflecting it. The amount of positive effort required to counteract that negative belief will be overwhelming, until the belief is changed.

The scenarios of Jill and James are an example of how two children from the same family can create such different lives based on the perceptions and choices they make as children. These make their way into the LTM to become core beliefs, which eventually become subconscious. This LTM data continues to create powerful outcomes that work either for or against the conscious efforts of the people concerned.

A positive cycle works in perpetual motion, unless something so powerfully negative happens that it overrides the positive and the momentum turns towards the negative. When this is the case, a person has to regroup and redirect their thinking patterns towards the positive. Remember, the universe does not judge, it only responds to our thoughts, so the strongest responses from the universe are due to the most powerful thought patterns.

Negative Core Beliefs

Covert negative core beliefs are difficult to uncover and part of us does not want to discover them. Children will suppress the negative beliefs, attitudes, and emotions that get them into trouble or that don't contribute towards them *feeling safe*. As we grow up, this becomes a habitual way of managing negatives. If we suppress a negative for long enough, then it will move below our conscious awareness, becoming a subconscious belief that can easily be denied. Self-denial is one of our greatest enemies. There are so many people with good, loving intentions and awareness who have dark, negative subconscious beliefs sabotaging their spiritual evolution.

Here is a major truth: The bigger the negative, the greater the charge it will have. The greater the charge, the more we will try to control it. We do this by avoiding thinking about it, by substituting negative thoughts with positive ones. We can suppress the negative until we're in denial that we have it at all. Problem solved! Except that, when triggered by certain thoughts or experiences, it shows its ugliness once again. If completely subconscious, it can become like a runaway train, out of control and free to covertly sabotage our life. Negative core beliefs ruin people's lives in some cases.

But we can uncover a negative core belief by monitoring our feelings and emotional reactions when the belief is challenged. How much we deny or defend is a clue to the strength of the belief's charge. Some people feel angry when challenged about a negative core belief. They believe that exposure is humiliating and that their image is under threat. They identify an element of their self-worth with the belief. The charge can be so strong that they may go on the attack to deflect the perceived onslaught. Overreaction is a sure sign that we have a very strong emotional charge on the subject.

To sum up, the emotions triggered when a belief is challenged will tell you how much charge you have on the subject. The more charge you have, the more out of balance your personal truth is in relation to the highest truth. Don't deny it. We can only heal something once we own that we have a problem.

Stress and the Survival Mode

We automatically go into survival mode when we are under stress, operating according to the information held in our LTM, bypassing the creative part of our brain and our ability to reason, and making us do what we have always done. Change does not happen easily when we are under stress. Most humans who live in modern society are under stress most of the time. Many people would like to create a better life for themselves, but if they are unhappy, then they also feel stress, which makes it very difficult for them to change. We need to get creative if we want to change our life for the better. Most people are so preoccupied with survival that they are not in a position to activate their creative brain. This is a Catch-22, because if people want to change then they have to first reduce their stress, but they are too stressed out to take steps to relax. Just to think of change is stressful for some people. Overcoming stress is not easy.

There are two forms of motivation: *inspiration* and *desperation*. If inspiration does not grab you, then hope that desperation does. The universal laws that control energy create these two motivational forces in our life. You can absolutely trust that if you are not moving towards being more positive in any area of your life, then you are moving towards the negative. If people don't do anything about their negativity, then it builds until they eventually become so desperate that they find the energy to change for the better. Being out of balance is very tiring. The further we move out from the line of balance, the greater the energy required to stay there. We eventually get tired of trying to maintain that out-of-balance state and want to be balanced again.

Using the Third Brain

The first stage of our brain's development gave primitive humans the ability to survive. The second stage allowed us to feel more emotion and to express ourselves more. Punishment and reward also came along, as did the early stages of clearer judgement about right and wrong. The third stage of development facilitated creativity and abstract thinking, which took creative thinking to a much higher level. Our long-term memory also developed and with it we could explore, record experiences, and more easily recall them at a later date. It is one thing to know how to do something but is another thing to know why. The third brain allowed us to explore and understand our spirituality in a more mature way, and we need to use it when we develop our spirituality.

We gain knowledge and then we apply it to deepen our understanding. Analyzing the new understanding allows for wiser, more educated decisions and expands our perceptions. We increase our consciousness, because we become more aware of who we are and our relationship with creation.

If we are under any type of stress at all, then we will use our first brain, where the basic functions are about survival first and rely on our LTM data for information. The first brain does not question the LTM's data and, therefore, it will act out whatever we have fed into it. Creativity and change do not happen in the first brain. The saying "monkey see, monkey do" implies that by repeating our old habits, we humans do the same and will continue to unless we use our creative third brain to change the pattern.

The human body is basically programmed to conserve energy by not doing anything unless the brain activates it—and if we don't use it, we lose it. If parts of our body are not being used positively and are not in a state of homeostasis (health), then they will be breaking down (in decay) as their energy moves towards the negative. It is the same with our mind and brain. Operating according to our programming takes less effort than using our creative brain to do something new. If we don't create spiritual change by using our mind/brain activity, then we will do what we have always done.

EXERCISE 6: CHANGING BELIEFS

This exercise is about changing an old, unwanted belief into a new, desired one. Subconscious negative thought patterns slowly accumulate and increase in power, affecting our health and well-being and our whole future, including anything that we try to consciously create. More importantly, they have a major effect on our spiritual evolution. We cannot ever completely remove original information (the core belief). However, we can reduce its impact by removing its charge. We then create an opposite, positive charge and embed that in our long-term memory. The aim of this exercise is to identify the problematic thought patterns and then to be prepared to face them, knowing that you can change their impact. You no longer need to fear, avoid, or deny them, nor suppress the fear-based emotions that they generate.

In advance of practising the exercise, identify a minor negative issue you wish to change. A problem that does not cause too much emotional pain is easier to erase from your long-term memory than something that holds a lot of charge. When you have success on a small issue, you will likely feel more confident that this exercise will work for a larger issue. Once you have recognized the negative energy associated with a particular belief, decide on the opposite positive that you want to embody. Practise conjuring the positive in your mind so that you can easily recall it during the exercise. Much effort and emotion needs to go into embedding a new belief. The success of this exercise depends on how committed you are to change. Do not feel guilty or judge yourself for having the negative. Feel good that you have enough self-love and power to face and change it. Then take the following steps:

1. Recognize a negative thought and the accompanying emotion. Allow the negative to live, by feeling it or expressing it in a responsible way. Own it rather than fear it. (After all, it is a part of you whether you accept or deny it.) This puts you in charge of your emotion instead of it being in charge of you. In other words, the emotion starts to lose its hidden power over you once you own it.
2. Choose a new positive for how you want to think, feel, or be. The positive needs to be the opposite polarity and of the same intensity as the negative thought/emotion that you're replacing. Using your imagination, allow yourself to feel the new emotion. Feeling the positive emotion is the key to creating the new belief. The more you feel the new emotion, the more powerful the change will be. You might exaggerate your new belief in order to activate more positive emotion and energy. Remember to keep it realistic or believable.
3. Choose to change. Go back to thinking and feeling the negative thought/emotion. Take control by using your

own authority. Say, out loud: "I now stop thinking (feeling, acting, and so on) like _____." (Fill in the blank with your particular negative. Feel the negative emotion for ten seconds or more.)

4. Next, say, out loud: "I now choose to think (feel, act, and so on) like _____." (Fill in the blank with your particular positive. Feel the positive emotion for ten seconds or more.)
5. Repeat steps 1 to 4 several times. You will notice that the negative starts to lose its power. It will get a little harder to find and feel as its energy lessens.

What happens when you face your fear? You are actually seeing through the illusion that it is real. Avoiding it gives the fear power over you. Facing it gives you power over the fear. The energy associated with the negative core belief lessens and the energy of the new belief is reinforced each time you repeat steps 1 to 4.

Remember, the more emotion you activate, the quicker the results will be. Eventually, the power of the new belief will be stronger than that of the old one. When it is, you will be automatically acting and reacting from the new, positive belief that you have instilled in your long-term memory. You may still feel the negative from time to time, but it will have lost its impact.

How long does it take to override an old, negative belief system? It depends on how strongly it is embedded in your long-term memory, how much effort you put into erasing its negative energy, and how deeply the new, positive belief is embedded in your long-term memory.

With this exercise, gradually work your way up to really big issues. The greater the fear, the more confidence and courage you will need to overcome it.

Phobias

Please note, this exercise is not recommended for strong phobias. You have to be the judge of whether you can work through an issue, and for some, professional help may be required. This exercise does, however, have the potential to work for some mild phobias. The information associated with a phobia will be heavily embedded in the long-term memory, so to address it, you can expect doing many repetitions of steps 1 to 4 to change it. You may find it too emotionally unsettling to face the full fear at the start; therefore, in the early stages, you may have to trigger small amounts of the negative memory. Very slowly, increase the amount of fear you invoke in step 1, and do not face more fear than you can handle. Be gentle with yourself and you may be able to overcome your fear. It is really important to remember that you created your phobia to survive a very extreme and fearful situation. In that context, the action was a positive.

6

Raising Our Consciousness

• • • • • • •

The two energies that affect our vibration are our thoughts and heart energy (love).

WE MAY be able to live a good spiritual life by connecting with our Creator through prayer, meditation, expressing love, or doing loving deeds, and so on. All these actions that come from within are expressions of our spiritual consciousness and reflect our level of spiritual growth. As do all actions, they use energy. They don't, however, increase the level of the vibration behind that energy. Many people think that they can reach divinity by doing loving acts, but, in fact, these are merely expressions. The level of consciousness that produces them is the true measure of our spiritual evolution. We spiritually evolve by increasing our vibration. Our thoughts and love energy affect our overall vibration. Pure, high-vibrating thoughts contribute to our heart's ability to generate pure love, which brings our vibration closer to that of our Creator. Therefore, our mind, brain, and heart relationship has a huge influence on our spiritual evolution as well.

If we learn something positive from expressing ourselves through an act, then the knowledge gained from the experience can contribute to an increase in our vibration, but it is not the act itself that creates the boost. For example, if we feel good about doing a kind deed, then the feeling good may help us see ourselves in a better light. If that increases our self-love, our heart will increase our vibration. If the self-love is temporary, then the increase in our vibration will be temporary as well.

Spiritual growth comes from being, not doing. If you are love, then you can act as love. Many people focus on doing loving acts for others and forget to fill themselves up with self-love first. One spiritual law states, "Love thy neighbour as thyself." If you love yourself first, as the law states, then you will find it easy to love others. If you focus on loving others first and neglect yourself, then you will end up looking for love from outside of yourself, too, having depleted your own reserves of self-love. Continually doing loving acts to feel good is doing it backward. When we have self-love, we are naturally drawn towards doing loving acts.

EXERCISE 7: MEASURING YOUR RESERVES OF LOVE

This exercise is about observing how you react to love from others. It teaches you about your state of self-love. In the following three scenarios, pay attention to your thoughts, feelings, and actions. You may wish to record your observations.

1. Notice how you think and feel when you are on the receiving end of love.

2. Recall a situation in your life when you have been with someone who shows you a lot of love and then switches it off.
3. Observe the ways that you seek love from others and how you show love to yourself.

Doing this simple self-reflection will tell you a lot about how full or depleted your reserves of love are. It is normal to feel good about being on the receiving end of a loving act. How much the act affected you will be your measure. If you enjoy the love and can then move past it, your reserves are likely somewhere between reasonable and high. However, if you enjoy it and then compulsively want more or feel flat, it is highly likely that you're looking for love outside yourself to top up your reserves. A person with healthy self-love does not need love from outside to feel good. They can enjoy the experience and then let it go.

If you get hurt when someone shows you love and then switches it off, you can be reasonably sure they were filling a hole within you. Most people would feel some sort of negative reaction. However, somebody whose self-love is fully topped will not feel anything negative, such as emptiness. A person at this high level can express unconditional love, because they don't need anything in return. Very few people can hold this amount of self-love for very long. These people usually display humility and balance, along with an inner strength that may not be that obvious to others until it is called upon. Most people look for love outside themselves to some degree.

If you *yearn* for more love from somebody, then you have not yet learned to fully give it to yourself. It is almost certain that you have a core belief that underlies the lack of self-love. It was most likely downloaded into your long-term memory (LTM) when you were very young and it continues to contribute to this negative state. Becoming aware of it is the first step towards changing it.

Some people are so wounded that they don't trust that anybody could really love them. Their own reserves of self-love are almost depleted. It is a very hard road back to self-love from there, but it can be done, usually with a lot of support and guidance from those wise enough to come from a state of compassion and not sorrow or pity. All negative states can be healed because the positive potential (the opposite polarity) exists as well. The same principle applies to the amount of energy required to create more self-love. For example, a recently developed minor negative belief about yourself probably does not have much amplitude. Therefore, a small amount of positive energy will be required to counteract it.

Extreme or prolonged negative energy creates the need for extreme and prolonged positivity to balance it out (healing can shorten this process). Everyone has the potential positive energy to overcome extreme negatives. What we need is the will, commitment, and information for achieving it, along with endurance, because balance very rarely happens quickly.

Our core beliefs from childhood have been accruing similar energies and beliefs throughout our lives, and we need to respect them. It is not reasonable to think that there is a quick fix for permanent change. Change is usually achieved through practice and commitment over a long period of time. Big issues may require outside support, such as group or individual therapy. It can take many years to fully expose and then overcome some extreme negative beliefs. The most common way to reach the belief is to start at the surface and slowly, methodically work through the layers, continuing until the deeply hidden core is reached. It's like peeling the layers off an onion. Every time a layer is removed, a deeper layer is exposed.

That may sound almost overwhelming to some people, so

what could be the motivation for those who want to change? It may come from being inspired to be a better person or from being desperate to overcome emotional pain. But motive is not as important as a positive step in the right direction. The alternative is to do nothing and continue to suffer. Achieving self-love is a step-by-step process. Each step brings us closer to the goal and further from where we don't want to be. The first steps are the hardest but the rewarding experiences of increasing our reserves of self-love keep us going.

THE BIGGER PICTURE

Expanding our mind and seeking ever-higher understandings leads us towards greater wisdom as we continually see an ever-growing "bigger picture." When this bigger picture is fully expanded, we have a taste of enlightenment in that area of our consciousness. We will see all! How do we know if we're seeing the biggest picture possible? The short answer is, we probably don't know for sure. We must accept where we are and be open to any higher truths coming into our awareness. Our spiritual journey is never done and we are always learning. We need to realize this and always be prepared to have our truths challenged. If you feel that your truth is threatened, then it is not the highest truth possible. The highest truth on any subject stands up to all scrutiny.

Judgement

Judgement is a necessary human quality that enables survival, but it can also be one of our biggest obstacles to attaining higher levels of consciousness. We make hundreds of judgements daily, many intended to keep us safe. Judgements are a normal part of our third-dimension experience and they belong here on the earth plane of existence. The highest truths, however, are all-encompassing and part of the omni-energy, in which everything is one and judgement does not apply.

Opposite polarities create conditions for comparison and judgement. Something is either one or the other, and there are no "in-betweens." They are direct and absolute opposites—for example, up/down, good/bad, right/wrong, day/night, black/white, love/fear, positive/negative—and ultimately (in the highest levels of awareness) neither is better or worse.

Here is an example of how, in order to understand an in-between, a greater level of consciousness is required. The colours black and white are relatively easy to identify, even for very young children. But a child needs slightly more mental maturity to understand that the colour grey is a combination of black and white and that it has a variety of shades.

Grey occurs frequently in our legal system, which is built around the presumption that the final verdict of guilty or not guilty is accurate. Lawyers present cases aimed at trying to prove guilt or innocence. The judgement is supposed to be based on the evidence alone, but some people are judged to be guilty, regardless of the facts. In-between evidence is open to interpretation—and misinterpretation. Individual perception can obscure the black-and-white evidence so that grey is what's seen instead. In such situations, a verdict based on the truth becomes difficult to deliver.

In the same way, because not everything is as obvious as black and white, our judgements are not always accurate. But to find our divinity, we need to learn *not to judge*—which is difficult for the average human. Judgements belong in the third dimension, and so do not serve spiritual issues. Our spiritual journey would be a lot simpler if its challenges were as clear as black and white. Despite our being driven to apply third-dimension judgements to it, the spiritual path is one of many grey shades. If we want to seek our divinity by raising our spiritual consciousness, then we need to elevate our thinking above the third dimension and leave judgement behind.

Judgement in the Third Dimension

The current consciousness of the human race is based on judgement associated with opposite polarities. Most, if not all, of our institutions, including our religions, are built around this concept. Religions cater to those living in the third dimension, where right and wrong, good and bad, holiness and evil, love and fear prevail. Likewise, many conceptions of God are one of a God of judgement.

The word *sin* describes an act that is contrary to God's laws. The Christians have the Ten Commandments, which are a set of God's rules to live by. To break any of these laws is a sin. However, people can be forgiven for their sins if they are truly repentant, and in different factions of Christianity, the clergy has ways of offering redemption. It would seem to be a black-and-white issue. If a person breaks one of God's laws, they can be forgiven if they repent. But what happens if they keep repeating the same sin? Can they always be forgiven? Spiritually, this is a grey area.

Usually, the reason why people repeatedly offend is that they have embedded in their subconscious a core belief that triggers negative behaviour. It may be so ingrained that it is like a compulsion, similar to an addiction. It was most likely planted in their LTM through an emotionally powerful, negative experience in their early childhood. For example, many adult bullies were themselves bullied during childhood. Many aren't aware of the abuse they experienced, because the memory is buried deep in their subconscious. They act out what they know and they may even think that their behaviour is acceptable. In most extreme cases, no amount of forgiveness offered by religion redresses the behaviour. Even the threat of penalties at the hands of the justice system does not dissuade. From what we know about subconscious LTM data, the core beliefs remain until they have been dealt with.

The potential to change all negative beliefs exists and it is imperative to our spiritual evolution that we learn to do this. Raising the vibration of our consciousness also includes changing those negative subconscious thought patterns that hold our vibration down. Our thoughts and the love in our heart, rather than our actions, are the two contributors to our vibration. We begin by purifying our thought patterns, including subconscious thoughts, because doing so purifies our love. The purification of these energies is paramount to reaching the highest levels of spiritual consciousness. If a person tries to love while having very negative thoughts, that loving energy will be weak and its impact will be short-lived. Enlightened beings are pure in thought and love. It is also said that love is the way to God.

When we move into the higher planes of awareness, we rise above the earth-plane concept of opposite polarities. We leave right and wrong behind and start to perceive levels of truth, where black and white are two extremes, with many shades of grey between them. Such perception is a quantum leap forward in our awareness. We come to understand that everybody is experiencing life from their personal level of truth. Some levels are more consciously advanced than others, but everybody does the best that they can according to their truth in their own spiritual evolutionary journey. Where does our personal level of truth come from? From the data held in our LTM, where our beliefs and perceptions are derived.

How can we judge anyone for living their level of truth? It is best to take the perspective that we, ourselves, have been there at some point in our past. We can observe their actions and attitudes and note how we feel about them. We can seek a feeling of compassion for others, rather than feeling sorry for them, because pity does not serve them but serves only to justify their situation. It does nothing to inspire change. Tough love knows no sorrow: It has understanding and offers inspiration to show the way out. It never imposes its will onto others, because that would violate the right to exercise free will. How can we blame someone for having sexual issues if they were raped as a child? How can we blame someone for not being able to love if they have never experienced love? How can we judge someone for always feeling like a victim when they grew up in a family that knew only victimhood? There is a higher purpose to everything, and we will probably never know another's reasons unless we make it our business to understand them.

Humans commonly try to prove what is right and wrong by arguing a point. This approach is ego-based and belongs in the third dimension. Powerful and clever minds can win a debate, but that does not make theirs the highest truth; it just means that they were the most convincing. One way to seek the truth is through discussion that allows for all points of view while keeping an open mind. This means abstaining from judgement until the discussion is complete. Then, making a judgement call is acceptable, but we need always to keep in mind that a higher truth may still be out there.

EXERCISE 8: SEEKING HIGHER TRUTHS

To seek our divinity by gaining more knowledge and understanding, we need to activate our mind. For this exercise, you may want to focus on being a better person, on creating better relationships with others or God, or on a spiritual teaching about which you have some doubt or confusion. You might explore the concept of a universal mind as a replacement for the common belief that we all have individual minds. Any understanding that develops your self-love will increase your vibration.

1. Set the intention of exploring a particular area of your spirituality, thinking about what specifically you want to explore.
2. Search for new information and compare it with current beliefs that you hold in your LTM. (You may need to research beyond your usual and accepted sources.)
3. Keep an open mind at this stage, because any judgement about something being right or wrong is influenced by our bias and can hinder or block the process.
4. Compare any new information with what you already believe. Observe the different data to see what makes more sense. How conclusive is this information and do you need to gather more?
5. Refrain from making any final judgements. It is natural to feel the need to be right, because most people identify their self-worth with being right.

If you experience a strong emotional charge, then you can be almost certain that it is being triggered by your LTM data. If part of a belief is feeling threatened, then it is not the highest truth, because the highest truth is never threatened. Sit with that emotion and let it pass. Try to recognize what is causing the emotional charge. Most people identify their self-worth with what they believe. No matter how hard we try, our bias will affect our intention of keeping an open mind. Bias favours our current beliefs. Be aware that it is present and influencing your thinking. Regularly evaluate whether you are stressed, as this will potentially close down your creative thinking and cause you to resist change. Be proactive and very involved in expanding your spiritual knowledge and understanding.

In this exercise, you can expect to have different and conflicting information and points of view. This is a normal and necessary part of the process. Move on and don't get preoccupied with trying to come up with an immediate answer. Seeing the bigger picture may require more information. Your current beliefs may be associated with a very high truth. If that is the case, this exercise is still beneficial, because it allows your current belief to be tested—and it will probably be reinforced and become stronger.

We need to allow our beliefs to be regularly tested and reviewed. You may eventually come up with a higher understanding, if you allow change to be an ongoing process. As your awareness increases to higher levels so your thoughts become purer. Pure thoughts have a huge effect on the love that comes from your heart. Together, they will increase your overall vibration.

You will reach times in your life where the information you hold on a particular subject will make perfect sense and you can say to yourself, "This is my current truth, as this is what I believe at this time." This statement allows for future information to influence your current thinking, for you to be engaged in an ongoing process of being open to new beliefs. This is a major tool to use in helping you raise your vibration.

7
Levels of the Mind

Understanding the origins of our thoughts.

WHAT DOES it mean to be a human being? Probably many things to many people.

Here is one description intended to provide an understanding of both the physical and spiritual aspects of being human: We are who we think we are. This statement encapsulates the idea that we are the expression of the levels of our minds, how we see ourselves, and our purpose. Some people see humans as only the physical or the ego self. Others relate to humans as the physical and spirit self. A few people see humans as having a physical, spiritual, and higher self. Such people see the complete human being.

THE MIND

The mind facilitates our consciousness, imagination, perception, recognition, reasoning, judgement, thinking, and memory. It is the centre that generates our thoughts and processes our feelings and emotions. It is also responsible for our attitudes and actions.

Another way of understanding the mind and its purpose is to see it as a tool. The mind has several levels and it can receive information and instructions from any of those levels but from only one level at a time. The mind can move information from one level to another. For example, it could receive information from a very high level and deliver it to our conscious awareness via an insight, idea, or feeling. We often think that this high-level information was our feeling or idea, but in fact we also receive information from other sources.

We usually think of ourselves as individuals who are separate from the whole, with thoughts that are ours alone. We may claim that we have control over our thoughts and what we do with them. However, we have no conscious control over blocking thoughts that come from the higher levels. We not only have universal information that flows through all of us, we also receive specific information that is relevant to us as unique individuals. For example, personalized information can be sent to bring something into our awareness (what we often call our sixth sense). We also receive high-vibrating information intended to help or guide us (sometimes called pearls of wisdom). Many people believe these insights are generated in our own mind. The truth is that we can think and act as individuals, but we're inseparable from the whole and we cannot block higher information from coming our way. Our choice is in how we interpret the information and what we then do with it.

We cannot experience or identify with the mind through our five senses (sight, smell, touch, hearing, and taste). The mind resides in our energy field, which we cannot see or feel but which encompasses our physical body. We can only experience the mind by its functions and by the results of those functions, which manifest in our actions, thoughts, and outcomes of those thoughts. Much research about the mind and its functions is influenced by the scientific way of understanding it. Psychology tends to focus on the mental, human levels of the mind, or the "human first" approach. The spiritual or "spirit first" approach is that we are spirits living in a human body.

The most accepted approach is human first, which requires proof that we are anything different or greater than what we appear on the third dimension to be. Many in the religious and New Age movements take this perspective. They generally think, "I am human and I have a spirit," as opposed to, "I am a spirit and my body is my human vehicle, which I need to experience life." They may believe in the spirit first perspective but live life as human first. Mainstream thinking often ridicules the spirit first approach. The human first approach hinders people's ability to comprehend how information from the Creator travels down through the levels of the mind until it reaches the ego level, where we become aware of it. The lower-level consciousness of the ego is generally not spiritually developed enough to recognize where this higher information comes from so its importance gets overlooked or, perhaps, ignored. This higher information continuously flows in from the universe regardless of people's ability to understand or acknowledge it.

The spirit first approach accepts that there are much higher levels to the mind. The psychological approach gets more recognition because it relates to the lower levels of the mind, which most people are familiar with. They know and can experience that their thoughts come from their mind. However, many people don't consider how those thoughts came into being. Some believe that their mind is the initiator of all their thoughts. They may say, "I wonder where that thought came from," but not investigate it. In fact, the higher dimensions feed information into our higher mind and it descends to the lower levels of our awareness. The more aware or conscious we become, the more we can recognize and interpret the information that flows into our mind.

The levels of the mind can be categorized into two parts that encompass all levels of our consciousness. An imaginary line separates the higher vibrations of the higher self from the lower vibrations of the lower self. These levels exist within our energy field and, therefore, they have access to our mind. (Please note, other models also describe different levels of consciousness; for example, the subtle bodies referred to in some Eastern traditions.)

THE HIGHER SELF/LOWER SELF MODEL

Higher self	Higher consciousness	Higher mind
	Imaginary line	
Lower self	Lower consciousness	Lower mind

Higher Consciousness

Higher consciousness refers to the levels at which we know we are connected to all that is and, therefore, are not separated from the source. Although higher consciousness contains different levels, each has the awareness that it is not individual or separate from the whole. "Higher self" is a term for all the levels of consciousness that exist above the imaginary line. It is the part of us that connects to our higher mind. The consciousness of I AM, the soul essence, and the highest vibration of all—the divine self—exist here.

Lower Consciousness

Lower consciousness refers to the levels at which we think of ourselves as individuals and, therefore, separate from the whole. These levels vibrate at lower levels, within the parameters of the third dimension, and belong to the lower self. There are two main levels in this section:

Spirit Self

Spirit Self is the highest-vibrating form of the lower self, generally more conscious than the ego self (described below). All the information that descends to the lower mind passes through and is processed by our spirit self before going to our ego self. Our spirits have lived many lifetimes in the third dimension. They will continue to reincarnate until they raise their consciousness to higher vibrations that no longer align with this earth-plane reality but with higher forms of consciousness experienced in other dimensions.

Ego Self

The lowest-vibrating form is our ego self, which we know as our physical self. Its role is to engage in life so that the higher levels can experience whatever manifests here. The ego level of the mind receives information and directions from the higher levels of consciousness in our field. Most people spend nearly all their time living in the ego level of consciousness—and need to, in order to participate in this world. The ego level of the mind is responsible for bringing information into our awareness. It creates thought patterns of which we can be conscious. It does this by interpreting and then processing the incoming information. The process involves an interaction between our mind and brain to ponder ideas, make decisions, and create outcomes. This is the level at which higher information manifests into reality so that our whole being can experience what we have created. The creative process and its outcomes may be the result of a lower mind-brain interaction of the ego, or it could be the result of higher information filtering down to the lower levels and manifesting into reality.

As we slowly become more aware of our higher self, we start to detect that higher information is penetrating our mind and that higher vibrating information flows throughout the universe. We become alert to the specific messages designed to support and guide us on our journey to becoming fully aware of our God Self. It is a step-by-step process that can't be bypassed. Each level has to be mastered before we are aware enough to tackle the next level.

The highest level of the mind will detect the purest information, while the lowest level's perception will be the most distorted. The distortion is caused by interpretations at the different levels, which are affected by the respective beliefs at that level. We can become aware of the higher vibrating information as it penetrates the upper levels of the mind. Imagine how much easier life would be if we could tune in to higher truths before they get distorted by lower beliefs. We could receive guidance in its purest form and avoid confusion about what it means. This distortion and confusion are the norm for most of us.

Confusion happens in the mind, often when a higher truth clashes with a belief that we hold. How many times have you had an idea and felt confused about what to do? Perhaps it seemed like a great idea, but then doubt crept in. You ended up doing nothing, because you had conflicting ideas and indecision. Let us reflect on what just happened here: The idea is received at the lower conscious level, where there is the mind, brain, and long-term memory (LTM) process. Here, your belief system gets involved, and so your idea is influenced by your life's experiences.

Another way to see this is that higher truths enter and your lower-self mind processes them, such that your personal truths influence that higher information. Most people will stay with what they already know and so the lower self decides on the safest choice. When higher truths conflict with personal truths, our personal truths usually prevail. People do what they have always done and that is one of the main reasons why our spirits have come to the earth plane so many times. When will we learn to listen to our higher self? Unfortunately, it is not quite that simple. We can choose to become aware on the highest levels but we have to be ready for it, having wisdom and mastery of the levels below. There are no shortcuts on this journey. Our wisdom evolves from knowledge coupled with experience. Knowledge by itself can be very dangerous. Here is a clue that we are starting to think from our higher self. We let go of the concept of right and wrong and see levels of truth.

The Spirit/Ego Relationship
Although the spirit self is of a higher vibration than the ego self, it is below the imaginary line, because it sees itself as an individual spirit. If it did not, then the third-dimension reality (which includes individuality) would no longer be required and neither would its human vehicle. Contrary to what many people think, our spirit is not our highest vibration. It is evolving, becoming more conscious of who it really is and finding its potential. The consciousness of a person's ego is directly connected to the consciousness of that person's spirit. The spirit cannot manifest and so it needs the ego to be able to experience its truths and discover how balanced those truths are when compared with the universal truths.

The spirit uses the ego self as a tool with which to experience life. We can choose to focus on the human first perspective, or we can focus on living from a spirit first perspective.

It's entirely up to us. The former is highly likely to keep us repeating life in the third dimension. The latter will start to open the gates to higher consciousness—and, doing so, will take us out of our comfort zone. The choice of the majority is to stay with the human first concept, living without having their beliefs being challenged. What do you want to do?

Because the mind is situated in our energy field, it receives incoming information in its pure form. Information from anywhere in the universe has the potential to penetrate our mind, which does not interpret that information until it travels to lower levels. The vibration of our overall energy field protects us from lower vibrating energies in the universe. A healthy field is the result of a loving mind and heart, and with these forms a strong, protective layer around our energy field that allows in only high-vibrating energies.

We have a responsibility to protect ourselves, because we can also weaken our field to a point where we lose the ability to filter out lower vibrating information. There are two main ways that we can allow these lower energies in—through fear and choice:

1. *Fear:* Fearful thoughts lower our vibration. An occasional or slightly negative thought pattern doesn't usually contribute to a breakdown in our field's protective layer. However, prolonged negativity and very fearful thought patterns, such as terror, can do great harm to our energy field. Another way to understand this is through the universal law of attraction: We attract what we are. If we live in fear, then we will attract more fear into our life. Our fearful thought patterns not only project into the universe (because that is what energy does), but they also weaken the protective layer of our own energy field. This can make us vulnerable to lower forms of energy and information penetrating our consciousness. This can create great confusion, because we normally don't know that we are

receiving lower energy and sometimes misinformation. We can get caught, without the ability to discriminate between truth and lie. It is up to us to find our way back into having a healthy energy field. There is only one way to do that. We need to clean up our negative thought processes and generate a high amplitude of love from our hearts.

2. *Choice:* We can deliberately or inadvertently choose to seek sources that weaken the protective layer of our energy field; for example, by using a Ouija board. (This practice has been known to wreck the lives of some people.) We can also open ourselves up by participating in some witchcraft practices, such as black magic. The universal laws protect our third dimension from being penetrated by lower energies. However, we can override this protection with our free will and choice, even if that choice is made out of ignorance or naivety. Universal law permits us to use our free will and choice however we like, which means we can form an agreement with outside forces that, once in, are very hard to get rid of. It takes a healer or spiritual person familiar with contracts and the relevant universal laws to break these agreements.

Humans generally don't know the power of the choices they make. These choices not only affect an individual's energy field, but they also have a real, if miniscule, effect on the entire universe. Powerful minds have a greater effect than weak minds, but all minds have the same potential. We each have to develop our own mind, for if we don't consciously control our mind then it will control us, and we need a disciplined mind to climb to the higher levels of consciousness. We all have thoughts that we'd rather not have. We need to deal with negative thoughts when we become aware of them. In the moment we become aware of negative thoughts, we can state the change we want to make. We need to reprogram the source of those thoughts by telling ourselves that we don't want them and how we do want to think. Self-talk is a very powerful reprogramming tool. It is also very effective if we correct ourselves immediately after we think, say, or do something that we did not want.

But we cannot change our thoughts when, because of an agreement, they are coming in from an outside source. Most agreements are formed when the lower-vibrating, outside force wants something from you and lures you in by pretending to help you or by giving you seemingly helpful information. If you have been caught up in one of these situations then you need to seek help from someone who knows what they're doing. Such an agreement is not something that an unspecialized person can change by themselves.

RELIGION, SPIRITUALITY, AND QUANTUM PHYSICS

Ancient art and records testify that humans have always been interested in spirituality. Their methods of transmitting this information existed long before humans learnt to write; for example, through artwork, dance, rituals, and storytelling. They were not scientific, but their methods were effective. We need to open our minds to the possibility that many common denominators connect ancient spiritual records, and some religious teachings and scientific research. The bridge between science and religion has been partly crossed with the relatively new discipline of quantum physics. Quantum physics is providing theories about how energy travels through the universe. Energy holds information. Everything is made up of energy and so life itself is subject to the information that energy holds. The way life is formed starts with information.

Western spiritual understandings point to God being the creator of everything. The three dominant Western religions generally believe that life exists because it is God's word or due to the will of God, and that life continues to exist through the grace of God. This is very like the understanding presented in this book, which is that *the creative force is responsible for the existence of all forms of energy and the life force is responsible for sustaining those forms.* If God changed Its mind and turned off the power supply, then nothing would continue to exist. Matter, along with all other forms of energy, would disappear in a flash, because the continual flow of information in the energy that allows it to exist would be no more.

The superstring theory of quantum physics offers an understanding of how this information travels through the universe. It attempts to describe all aspects of the universe by modelling them as tiny, supersymmetric strings. The superstring theory could easily be representing a highway of energy flow that holds all the information for life itself or that has a constant pattern and rhythm to it. Some in the New Age movement refer to this as "the rhythm of life." This is one example of many similarities between science, religion, and spiritual teachings.

The divide between religious and scientific approaches is mainly because religion is primarily based on unprovable, subjective information while science is based on provable, objective information. Religions totally rejected early science and branded scientists as charlatans and heretics, and put some to death. Science slowly gained more credibility, but the scars were not forgotten and the divide between the two still exists. The religious approach was dominant and religion the authority that science challenged. Now subjective, emotionally driven understandings have been eroded by objective, factual research. When the two institutions meet in the middle, science offers credibility to some spiritual teachings about creation.

Many people in the Western world no longer accept the reasoning behind religious authorities stating, "This is the word of God and it cannot be challenged." This position does not allow for us to use our discernment, wisdom, and right to question religious hierarchy. But we have a right and *duty* to challenge all concepts and teachings, which include those of religion and science. By doing so, we will continue to unravel the higher secrets of God and creation. We can be sure that the highest truths will always stand up to any scrutiny they are exposed to. True spiritual masters know they have to exercise their right to question any teaching or truth presented to them. They also know that the highest truth will always prevail. We owe it to our own spiritual journey to pursue the higher truths rather than solely believe what others tell us.

The model I'm presenting is based on the premise that we are our higher self, who has a spirit living in a human body. The mind helps facilitate our ability to operate on the physical plane and to connect with the highest levels of consciousness in creation. As a tool for us to use, the mind brings us back to the question: "Who are we?" Our understanding of what it means to be human can be as narrow or as wide as our level of consciousness will allow. If we think that we are only a physical human, then that is what we will experience. If we think that we are a spirit in a human body, then we will experience both being a spirit and a human. If we think that we are a higher self that is greater than our spirit or human body, then we will have the ability to experience all three levels, all of which have equal importance.

The mind creates thoughts and has a managerial role in directing the brain to function in certain ways. We need to use our mind on this human level to function properly in the third dimension. We cannot think or reason with our brain because, while it can operate without our mind and can respond to thought, it cannot create thought.

Our mind has the capacity to operate on different levels of consciousness and it responds to our awareness and intentions.

When our awareness is operating on the human (ego) level, the vibrations of our thoughts will reflect this. If we operate from our spirit level of consciousness, then our mind generates thoughts that reflect that level of vibration. We need to use the highest levels of our mind if we want to experience the highest levels of consciousness.

Information and the Mind

Energy and information constantly flow throughout the universe and all around us whether we are conscious of it or not. As our awareness increases, so does our ability to access higher levels of our mind. If we are not aware of the information that's steadily transmitted to us, it is not because we have a faulty antenna. It's because we haven't activated the pathways for moving the information from our antenna down to the current level of our mind. We have to become aware that these pathways exist before we can activate them.

As discussed above, as it descends through the levels of our mind, information gets filtered. Much is so diluted by the time it reaches our lower consciousness that we don't even notice its presence. Some people recognize little snippets of it but choose to ignore it anyway. Some people are so far removed from information in alignment with higher truths that they are almost completely cut off from the Creator. This begets a "chicken and egg" scenario. People need to open their awareness so that they can recognize that they're receiving higher information. However, because they don't experience receiving it, they don't see the point of opening up to something that they don't believe is there.

There is one saving grace relevant to the last scenario: Energy will eventually bring us back to the place we started. The higher spiritual truth is that we were created by our Creator and to our Creator we will return. God constantly sends us higher information to help us find our way back and this will never change. The only thing that can change is our ability to become aware of it, which starts by setting the intention to always open up our mind and training ourselves to think on increasingly higher levels. The higher the level we attain, the clearer the information we perceive.

Here is an illustration of how the flow of information passes from the higher realms down to the physical plane.

FROM GOD TO THE EGO

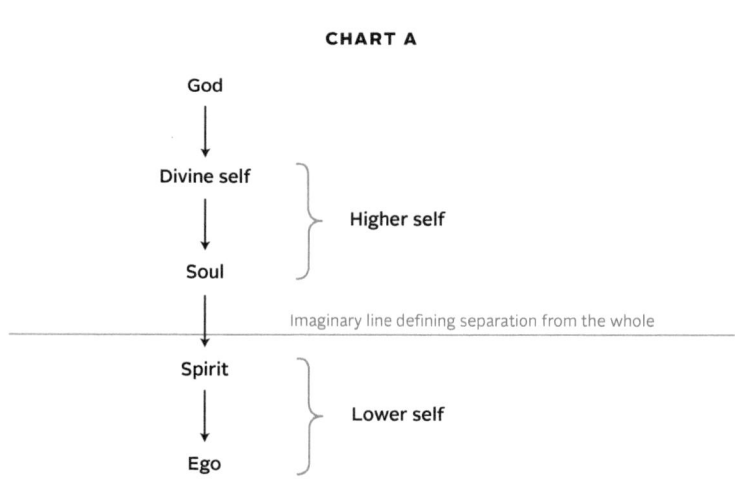

Chart A shows a model of how information filters down from God through the levels of our consciousness until it gets to the ego level. The imaginary line represents the divide between the two levels of awareness. One is the awareness that we are a part of the whole (above the line) and the other is that we are individual spirits who are separate from the whole (below the line). Note that this is the God flow and that the universal mind is not involved because God does not have a mind. We can receive information from the God source in several ways. It can be through intuition and feelings, an inner knowing. It can be through a sign (thus the saying, "It's a sign from God"). It can come into our mind through an idea, insight, or dream. This information comes directly to us and not via the universal mind.

FROM THE CREATOR TO THE PHYSICAL PLANE

Chart B shows a model of how information filters down from the Creator (the creative aspect of God) and the highest levels of universal consciousness to the physical plane via the universal mind.

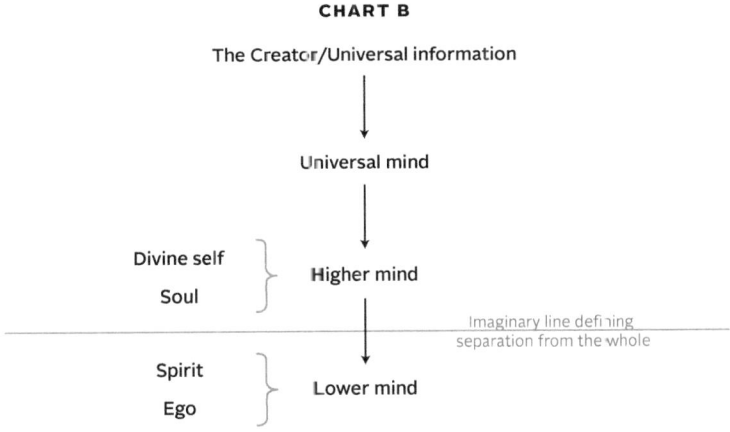

The information that flows our way from God in Chart A is pure because it is separate from the universal mind. All other information flows through the universal mind and it can come from anywhere. It is up to our personal ability to interpret the incoming information. We need to use our discernment in this process. The more conscious we are, the better we will be able to discern between the good and the bad, the useful and not so useful, the helpful and the deceptive information. There is no substitute for self-awareness when it comes to safely processing any information coming in through our mind.

Spirits

The main reason for almost every spirit's experiencing third-dimension reality is that their consciousness has not allowed them to move above the imaginary line as shown in the two charts on the preceding pages. There may be some or many ready to make the transition into the higher planes but they remain. Most spirits are struggling to master the earth plane experiences; otherwise, they would not have so many lifetimes on this plane. There is also the possibility that a spirit keeps coming back because it really enjoys this reality, although it is hard to imagine why. Although there may be rare exceptions, every spirit comes into this life with lessons to learn, life challenges to overcome, and skills to master. Spirits come into each incarnation with negative karma to work through. Very few are close to mastery, while many are still unaware of their higher purpose. Other spirits enter this dimension through agreements, and some have very negative intentions. The extremes of these intentions could be classified as evil.

There is another group of spirits who did not choose to leave this plane at the point of death. When we die, a window to the other side opens to allow the spirit through. This opportunity lasts for only a short period of time. Some choose not to cross over for one reason or another. These reasons are nearly always fear based. Once the window closes then they are stuck on the earth plane. They very quickly realize that they don't have a physical body to experience life and to manifest their thoughts and desires. They are often full of fear and sometimes very angry when they realize that they are stuck in the third dimension. These are what people call ghosts. They still have a mind because they have thoughts and can create outcomes. It is as though their etheric body is partially materialized. There are huge amounts of seemingly unexplainable sightings of these entities. A camera can capture their silhouette or etheric body. They move in spirit form manifesting outcomes. People see objects being moved, they hear footsteps and strange voices, and they sometimes see silhouettes. It isn't a myth that they like dark places and hang around certain spots, such as where they met their death. Many seem to be attracted to very negative energy. Plenty of evidence of these spirits exists.

Another category of spirits is of those who have come down to the earth plane to help with the transition of human consciousness into a higher plane. These spirits have volunteered to do this work out of love for humanity and the universe. They exist in physical form and have a normal body. The difference is that they are quite advanced at spirit level. Some are surprised about how hard it is to be human and to engage in the experiences that come with it. Many find it difficult to understand the negativity of human consciousness and feel like outcasts.

Our spirit is not fully evolved because it still has areas in its consciousness that need developing. It takes on different lessons and different challenges each time it comes back to earth. It will repeat this journey for as many times as are needed to become a master living to our full potential. Most spirits enjoy the power and choice that comes with being separate from the whole. Some don't want to give up their individuality by surrendering to the whole because they believe that they will be powerless and lost in the greatness of it all. They have emotions and so they can be happy or angry. They have a memory of their past and can use the mind to manifest their future. Spirits receive information from different levels of the higher self as well as from other sources. As this information travels down through the mind, the spirit processes it. The spirit's interpretations are passed down to the ego level of the mind, where the information is processed against the brain's LTM data (in other words, against what the ego already knows). Decisions are made at the ego level, expressing the information. Life is experienced in accordance with what the spirit self wants.

It is almost impossible to believe that some people have chosen such a difficult life. However, as hard as that is to comprehend, there is a higher purpose behind every experience. Much suffering is karmic. It is necessary to balance out a past-life negative. Someone who rapes or murders in this life will have to face a huge negative experience to balance out the energy or to learn their lesson in another life. Karma is not about punishment. It is an automatic consequence of action. The law of balance comes into play. Once the lesson is learned, then that spirit's consciousness rises above the need for more of the same experiences.

The Covert Negative Self

Another level of the mind needs to be mentioned because of its negative influence. The covert negative self exists in the mind as a very low vibration and could be seen as the lowest part of our lower self, the opposite polarity to the highest levels of our higher self. It consists of a very dense group of extremely negative thoughts that we have accumulated in the past and driven into our subconscious rather than healed or transmuted into higher vibrating energy. As you know, similar thoughts accrue and become more powerful than individual thoughts. Science calls this accumulation of thought-energy "memes." Memes have their own momentum and their consciousness can create outcomes. Some extremely negative thought patterns are hidden deep in the lowest levels of the mind and covertly work on their own agenda. Most people don't know that the covert negative self exists, and yet it is one of our worst enemies because it sabotages our life. The power and the level of sabotage depend on the amount of accumulated negative energy it holds, and the effects can sometimes be experienced as self-sabotage.

One way to uncover these negative thoughts is by revealing and healing our higher self mask. (We will explore this more in Chapter 10.) If you have trouble with how other people see you and think that you have healed all the associated negative conscious and subconscious areas of your mind and LTM, then you may have a negative self-sabotage playing out through your higher self mask. You do not need to fear this covert negative self, but you do need to respect and heal this aspect once you have reached a very high level of awareness.

The covert negative self is referred to as the "lower self" in the model used in the wonderful, channelled material presented by Eva Broch Pierrakos. (See https://pathwork.org/lectures/the-higher-self-the-lower-self-and-the-mask/.)

EXERCISE 9: IDENTIFYING THOUGHT VIBRATIONS

The exercise cannot be rushed, so please do it at your own pace. It is intended to increase your awareness of the level from which your mind generates thoughts. With practice, you will be able to sense the distinct vibrations of various thoughts. The higher the vibration, the higher the level from which that thought is generated.

Start by becoming aware of how an angry thought feels compared to a happy thought. Positive thoughts generally feel lighter and more enjoyable than negative ones do. Practise invoking very negative and positive thoughts and noticing the different sensations that accompany each. Once the distinction between the extremes is easy to detect, invoke less acute polarities until you can sense the difference in the subtler negative and positive energies. Then set aside some time to do the following:

1. Create a dialogue between your spirit and ego. Imagine that you are your spirit and ask your ego a question that requires an answer. Deliberately respond from your ego's perspective. Continue the conversation no matter how false it may feel. Closely observe any differences in the energy between the spirit and ego. You are the one playing out these roles, so you are actually observing yourself. Look for differing emotions, thoughts, reactions, and responses. Sense the difference between the two energies. The spirit usually feels lighter. Continue these dialogues between your spirit and ego. Over time, you will improve at recognizing the difference between the two.
2. After becoming familiar with the spirit and ego energies, set the intention to be your higher self. There is a sense of power about the higher self. It has a stronger presence than the spirit. Develop a dialogue between your higher self and spirit in the same way that you did above between the spirit and ego. You may find that your spirit does not recognize the higher self and this may be because your spirit didn't know that the higher self exists. Role play the dialogue between the two and see what develops.

Knowing that you are whatever you focus on, this exercise may help you to better understand the question: "Who am I?"

This exercise requires openness to whatever emerges. Though spirit is usually more conscious than ego, I have experienced one case, during a healing session, with a client who had a very angry spirit that was aggressive towards the ego. The ego was powerless to fight this energy and felt like a victim.

The energy of the ego actually felt better to the person than the aggressive energy of the spirit.

The first time I did this exercise, my ego became very self-conscious when it realized it could not hide from my spirit. It took a lot of reassuring from the spirit that it did not judge the ego before the ego felt safe and relaxed. As a result, about a week later, I noticed that I felt markedly more confident and people commented that my voice sounded different. I believe this was the outcome of the ego feeling safe and not judged.

When I began practising the second step, my spirit would not recognize my higher self. My spirit needed convincing of the new reality that my higher self was actually of a higher vibration. The spirit relaxed when it realized that it was not judged but was only supported by the higher self. Both steps of this exercise helped integrate all three levels and I felt more spiritually complete afterwards.

Intentions

Intentions create powerful energy and when we set an intention to do something, we trigger support from the universal energies. The higher the intention, the higher the level of support. High vibrating intentions attract high vibrating responses. They naturally go hand in hand, and we can trust that all responses will be governed by the universal laws.

You may have heard said of someone, "He has a lazy mind," but there's an inaccuracy in this statement. The mind is a tool to be used. It does not get up in the morning and say, "Oh, I think I will do nothing today because I just don't feel like it." This statement comes from the person using the mind. Sometimes we can't be bothered to think something through or about it at all.

That is us, not our mind. The mind is more like a computer program that will do whatever we want it to, so long as it is capable. We need to train our mind to operate the way we want it to be. We have control over nurturing and training it to work for us. The mind might seem lazy; however, it's the person controlling the mind who's lazy.

If we don't actively work on developing our mind, then it will shut down to the level that is required. Admittedly, some people have brilliant minds while others find it much harder to process information, but we all have the same potential. The reason why we all have different levels of mind performance does not necessarily have to do with activating and training it. For example, low performance may not suit one's higher purpose, or having a high intellect in this life may distract a person from an important spiritual lesson that they have come to learn. I am now sixty-eight years old and with the benefit of hindsight I can see the bigger picture of my life. Many experiences that I perceived as negative had a higher purpose and I can appreciate how they have helped mould the person I am today. I don't believe that I could have done what I have come to do if I had the brilliant mind of a scientist. I wouldn't have found the time to contemplate the higher purpose of life if I had been preoccupied with a hectic lifestyle. Take time to consider your own life and the reasons why your mind performs the way it does and make a decision about what you are going to do with it.

8

Universal Mind

· · · · · · ·

One mind, one consciousness.

THE MIND is the most important tool we possess. We need to develop a healthy mind if we want to have healthy spiritual and physical bodies, healthy relationships, love, peace, and harmony. Everything in our lives—our reality, our future, anything we create—all starts in the mind. *How we create and experience all life starts with the mind.* General education is mainly associated with the ego level of the mind and its relevance to the physical world. Our consciousness would evolve much faster if we included all the levels of the mind in our studies and if more emphasis was placed on understanding the functions of the complete mind.

ONE MIND

There is an all-encompassing higher truth, which is that there is only one mind: the universal mind. The universal mind has all the functions and qualities of mind that we experience on a personal level. But our personal level of mind is like a laptop, whereas the universal mind is like an enormous supercomputer. A laptop processes commands from its operator; a supercomputer is capable of receiving billions of signals from all operators at any given moment. Both computers are capable of processing information; however, one is limited and the other is unlimited or infinite. The universal mind can collect and process every thought of every human as they happen. It files the information in its memory and produces outcomes according to what's in the files. And the total number of human thoughts may be a very small proportion of all thoughts happening on all levels of consciousness throughout the universe. Add to this the possibility that some scientists postulate: There are multiple universes. Where does it end? Maybe there is no end—creation itself is said to be still expanding.

All consciousness is linked together through the universal mind. The old paradigm is still relevant for those who think that they are individuals (which includes most of the human race). We tend to believe we are individuals who have our own minds. This perspective does not accommodate the higher truth that we are all of one mind. However, a person who can see the reality that there is only one, omnipresent mind will also understand that the concept of individual minds exists as a lower truth. Higher truths can always accommodate lower truths, but lower truths cannot accommodate all the higher truths.

The "one mind" concept fits perfectly with the idea that there is only one consciousness. The terms Oneness, the whole, unified field, all that is, universal mind, and so on, all describe this phenomenon. The process of creation (the three stages of thought, word, and deed) applies to all levels, and all creation is a form of consciousness. This means that the mind creates consciousness. Let's return to the description of how creation started, described in Chapter 1: The void and the mind existed together. God emerged from the void, and an aspect of God is the Creator. Although God does not have a mind, the Creator has a mind. The Creator then created the consciousness that we know and experience. This means that the mind of the Creator was necessary for the creation of consciousness. This supports the statement that the mind precedes consciousness. In other words, the universal mind is what makes consciousness continue to exist.

Mind and Outcomes

Powerful minds create powerful outcomes. Many people find it hard to accept that there is only one mind and everybody can access all of it. We personally don't believe we have the capacity to activate the sheer magnitude of this massive "mind power." Our own thinking limits us. If we think from the ego level, then that is all we will experience. If we think from our spirit, then we will be limited by the belief that we're individuals with a discrete mind. When we become conscious of our higher self, we acquire the awareness of being part of something much greater. When we get to this level of consciousness, we can more easily comprehend the reality that there is one universal mind. This understanding brings a total respect for the universal mind's power along with a level of spiritual maturity that deters us from misusing even a miniscule portion of its power. Miracles can be performed by those who truly understand how to activate the higher vibrations of the universal mind.

An inbuilt safety factor protects us and the universe from individuals using more of this mind power than they can handle at both the positive and negative levels. The level of our vibration reflects our level of consciousness, and we cannot use the power vibrations higher than our own. We may try to access higher levels of consciousness (such as by meditating, praying, or concentrating), and sometimes we may succeed. However, the connection will last only as long as we are in that state of mind. It is very unusual to be able to hold that high state of consciousness while participating in daily life. Some people try to hold that higher state, but they often appear to be aloof and ungrounded. We need to be grounded to truly partake in the third dimension, which nearly all of us are here to master. We need to be grounded to manifest our ideas and thoughts.

An imaginative, creative mind is a great asset. We can dream about how we want our future to be and how we will feel when that becomes a reality. However, those dreams do not become reality unless we ground them by applying the three-stage creative process we discussed in Chapter 1. Some get to the second stage of the process (thinking, talking, planning) and then give up. They have not grounded their ideas by applying the third stage, which is the manifestation of the original thought. You have to apply the doing stage if you want to become what you want to be. You may know of people who have wonderful ideas and great plans but they never seem to bring them to fruition. Many people become victims of their own inaction and then blame the world around them for not achieving their goals. It takes awareness and energy to bring ideas into reality.

Dark Forces

Dark forces also have access to this universal mind, because it is a tool that responds to all levels of consciousness. Anyone who has worked in the healing area and who deals with these extremely negative beings will know how powerful their minds can be. They are masters at creating chaos and destruction wherever they can penetrate another vibration. Partly, they can use the power of the mind because they vibrate at levels that are hidden from most people's awareness. They covertly work away, unhindered where they create very negative outcomes. Nevertheless, the vibrations of the light will always be greater and more powerful than the vibrations of the dark side. It is possible to expose them to the light. A healer (or the like) needs to know how to work with the universal laws that allow these dark forces to operate. They cannot resist very high vibrating energy.

The majority of humans do not need to fear dark forces. Although if the vibration of a person's energy field drops low enough, they may be vulnerable to the influences of these dark forces. Anyone who travels towards the darkness has chosen this path either consciously or subconsciously. Dark forces have always been here and have access to the lowest levels of the universal mind. They are a necessary part of creation, because the light would not shine without the dark. The vibration of these dark forces is extremely low, and lower vibrations cannot penetrate higher vibrations unless they are deliberately or unintentionally invited in. But these forces are not to be feared, and the best way to protect ourselves from being penetrated by them is to focus on moving towards the higher consciousness of the light.

The universal mind generates thoughts, and thoughts are energy. Everything is composed of the same energy, all energy has consciousness, and all consciousness is created by this one mind. Everything in existence is connected and can communicate plus have an effect on everything else through this same mechanism. No matter how minuscule the effects of our thoughts, they still influence the rest of the universe. Everything can communicate with all else, and this potential is governed by the level of consciousness a being is operating on. How things interrelate depends on resonance between specific vibrations. For example, a rock has one of the slowest vibrations in creation, and so its effect on the rest of creation is one of the lowest. Humans have a much higher vibration than a rock and hence we have a much greater effect on creation.

Somebody with very negative intentions (or evil ones) will have a very low-frequency vibration behind those thoughts. They may also have a lot of anger, hatred, or powerful fear generating high amplitude, which can create devastating outcomes. But a high vibration with an equal amplitude will always override a negative. In other words, terror may be subdued a little by a weak form of love, but it can be eliminated by the fearless presence of an unyielding, high frequency and amplitude of love. The highest form of this love is God!

Past-Life Mastery

We might think that we should be able to read what the highest levels of the universe are thinking, but we can't. Something must stop us from doing that. Our purity of mind and the level of love in our hearts determine our overall consciousness. Those two factors control our ability to connect with other levels of consciousness. However, many philosophers and those with incredible scientific minds and skills probably did not have pure minds and hearts. How do we account for that? Some of the answers can be found in understanding the spirit, how evolved it is, and the purpose of its life on earth. Some aspects of our consciousness may be highly evolved because we have mastered them in a past life. Other aspects may be very unevolved and may even be very negative. If so, we know they have not been mastered.

This reality applies to some spiritual leaders as well. They present themselves as highly evolved and have attracted great followings of people who tend to be awed by their greatness and blindly follow like sheep, oblivious to the possibility of deception, lies, and cover-ups. These types of leaders are the great deceivers of this world. We have to be aware and use what wisdom we have when we turn to others for guidance.

The situations described in this chapter are among the big dilemmas for humanity. Most people look to others for guidance and protection. The way to higher consciousness requires us to take charge of our life and discover the truth for ourselves. We may draw on other people's wisdom, and then we must apply it to our life to know how it works for us. This is a slow process involving gaining an understanding, applying it to life, garnering wisdom from the experience, making new and higher choices, then applying them to life... And so, this cycle repeats as we move towards our true divinity. The higher we climb, the easier it becomes to access the highest levels of the universal mind.

9

The Blueprint

· · · · · · ·

The plan designed for our spiritual growth

A LOT OF information available about the higher purpose of our current cycle on earth is available. That we are born, we live, we die, and our existence ends does not make sense; nor does the belief that we have only one lifetime on earth and how we perform during it determines our future for eternity. It seems that we return to earth several times. Very strong evidence suggests that we all have a blueprint for how our life is meant to unfold and that this was written before we came to earth.

THE REVIEW BOARD

Let's examine our journey from when we existed in spirit form, before we took this trip to earth. Some believe that, before we depart, we meet with a "review board" consisting of very high and wise beings, similar to an annual review with our work colleagues during which we come up with a plan to improve our personal performance and develop the best way forward. We discuss where we are at in our overall spiritual journey and mutually agree on what we want to achieve during our next earth cycle. These are very high-level choices with very high vibrations. Everything is put in place to create the best potential for spiritual growth. The plan is very complex and comprehensive. The emphasis on spiritual growth may or may not incorporate happiness and peace on the physical level. We often encounter hardships and confront challenges designed to awaken our awareness. The whole plan includes everything from agony to ecstasy, depending on what we have chosen to experience. The ultimate aim is to increase our awareness of who we really are by being challenged to reach our highest potential in all areas of our life on earth.

The journey is about awakening our spirit and this overrides the desires for pleasures of the ego self. This plan is meant to be challenging. How else can we become a master if we don't have challenges to overcome? Mastery is achieved by the road less travelled—and it's a hard one. Humans naturally follow the path of least resistance, but God is not affected by this path because Its consciousness is greater and more powerful. At the human level, there are many situations in which we follow the path of least resistance, and nothing's wrong with that. If we want to become God-like, then we have to become greater than the resistance, too. (Our ultimate aim is to return to our source, which is to be with God.) The law of least resistance constantly pulls us back into complacency and drains our willpower. An extreme example is when people prefer to stay in bed rather than face the challenges each day presents. Unfortunately, another law of energy drags them further into their gloom: If you don't use it, you lose it.

We can call this plan our blueprint, and in its creation is a higher truth about our relationship with choice. This plan was made at spirit level and it was chosen out of many possibilities that were designed for the advancement of the spirit. We made major choices about what we would experience during this trip to the earth plane. The blueprint may be flexible to a point; however, it is unyielding in its purpose to create the best potential for spiritual growth. If we make a choice here on earth that is in conflict with the intention of the blueprint, then we will create conflict in our life. If we have conflict in our life because it's in the blueprint, then we can easily create more conflict and make our challenge harder than it needs to be. We can fight the direction the blueprint set by making other choices, but the forces driven by the blueprint will always pull us back onto our path. From this perspective, our ego-based choices may be interfering with our higher choices. That can be very confusing, so let's define the difference between the two.

We really can't permanently override our blueprint, because any choices we make that are in conflict with our spirit choices (captured in the blueprint) create an imbalance of energy. Because the choices made by the review board are of higher vibrations than those of the ego level, they create the greatest potential for balance. Therefore, the lower ego choices will eventually be overridden, because energy is always pulling us back to balance. Choices made on an ego level will create powerful, permanent outcomes only if they are in line with the blueprint.

The path of least resistance is achieved when our decisions are in alignment with our higher choices. The opposite occurs when our decisions are in conflict with our higher choices. Therefore, our decisions can make our life easier or harder than it needs to be. For example, let's assume that we have decided on a career that is in conflict with our blueprint. It will be very difficult to succeed in that career. There are many people who are not happy at their jobs. They get to an age (usually in midlife) when they seek change; some feel ready to pursue dreams they have ignored for a long time. Those are likely in their blueprints. Usually, the changes made are very satisfying and the new career is much more enjoyable and rewarding.

Ultimately, the spirit is most affected by our choices because it is the aspect that is spiritually evolving. Ideally, the spirit should be making the choices and the ego should enact them, so that the spirit can experience the consequences of its choices.

God only observes what It has created. It experiences the outcome of Its creations in the same way that we experience the results of ours. (Again, this is an example of the hologram.) God does not judge, punish, or favour, because everyone was created equal. Some people seem to be very lucky in life. Others may envy them and think they are blessed, that God favoured them. But what seem like favour and punishment are really the consequences of past actions. We reap what we sow! There is no luck. The terms good and bad luck may provide an explanation for inexplicable inequities, but everything has a higher purpose and there are no coincidences in the divine plan—it is perfect in every aspect. It is much easier to embrace life when we understand that truth. Even suffering has its place and higher purpose, although that truth may be almost impossible for a victim to comprehend. People who carry out atrocities in this life will experience what it is like to be on the receiving end at some point in a future life. This does not apply to all those on the receiving end of atrocities in this life, but it accounts for at least some. Karma often plays a big role in the more extreme hardships we endure.

The review board addresses areas of our consciousness that we have and have not mastered. Things that seem easy for us to master are clues to what we have mastered in a past life. These are also areas that we are drawn to or that offer the least resistance to our *positive* efforts. For example, some people have natural talents and areas of their life seem blessed. Either they have earned these or there is a deeper reason why they have such blessings. Likewise, either the incredibly tough hardships that some people face are a consequence of their past actions (karma) or a deeper positive reason underlies them. This deeper reason is often obscure and may take a lifetime to realize.

Astrology and Numerology
The consciousness of the planets has a huge effect on us, and the position of them at our exact time of birth sets up the basis of our personality, our qualities, and challenges plus the purposes and story of our life. One of the main disciplines for studying this complexity is astrology, and there is a huge amount of information to be examined, if we choose. It can take years to understand and apply the information available. Astrological charts can show us all our main attributes plus the main challenges and at what stages they will influence our life.

Numerology is another source of valuable information that provides similar knowledge to astrology. Numerology is associated with sound. Sound generates vibrations that an important part of creation. Any time that we sound out our full name (given at birth), we create a vibration in our personal energy field. This specific sound was in our blueprint and has an influence on our personality. For example, I grew up with a nickname. It was used so often that some people thought it was my real name. The year that I got serious about my spiritual journey, I also left farming and began a career in marketing. The change required moving to a new location, and I needed to use my birth name for business reasons. Nobody in my new environment knew my nickname and all addressed me by my birth name. My birth name activated the energy associated with my spiritual journey as was in my blueprint. Years later, I had my astrology chart done and it indicated that I had started my spiritual path at that time, which serves as confirmation to me that the timing of my name and career change was no coincidence. The names we are born with are no accident. Parents may think that they alone choose their child's name. However, the higher sources guided them to it. There may be exceptions to that rule, but they are very rare.

Palm readings may also provide information about your blueprint, although in my experience they are better for general information and confirming information from other modalities. Psychic readings may also provide some confirmation, likewise channelling and deep meditations. All may contribute to your confidence on your spiritual path.

Genetic Inheritance

Almost everything, particularly major events, is in our blueprint. This includes our genetic structure and inheritance. Genetic makeup starts forming during the three-month incubation period of an egg in a mother's ovaries. The environment the mother experiences at that time has an influence on the characteristics of the genes being selected. Some religions acknowledge the need for a prospective mother to remain safe and calm during this three-month period, believing that the environment a mother experiences pre-conception has a significant effect on the emotional and physical aspects of any future child. If this is true, then our spirit must be involved somehow.

One belief is that our spirit arrives close to the time of conception. The mother's environment also influences a development during the nine months in the womb. The relationship between the mother and the father (if he is around) has a major effect during pregnancy. A developing baby also responds to the environment, so this phase is more influential on the baby's makeup than the incubation period of the egg. The birth itself has another significant impact on some aspects of genetic potential. By the time we are born, there have been many influences on our genetic composition, and nearly all of them are in our blueprint. Most of our characteristics and potentials are now in place and we are still not old enough to make decisions about whether and how we will use them.

The next phase in our life involves a very fast learning curve and major downloading of information into our long-term memory (LTM). This is when most of our core beliefs are formed. It is interesting that we are not developed enough to discern between what information we want or don't want. We download experiences and accept them without choice. We are not old enough to make learned decisions for ourselves yet. We do not make major decisions that would interfere with our blueprint before the ages of four to seven. Our base personality, core beliefs, perceptions, and personal truths are in place before we are old enough to think for ourselves.

It may seem very unfair when we consider the inequalities of children's environments; for example, a child born into poverty and near starvation versus a child born into safety and luxury. It could be said, from an ego perspective, that we have no say in who we are, that we are the end result of forces outside our control. Whereas, from a spirit perspective, we are exactly who we planned to be and we are here because we want to be. Mothers often refer to their babies as little miracles. It is nothing short of miraculous that the course of life for that baby is perfectly designed for what the spirit needs.

Between the ages of four and seven, we learn to take control of our life. We start making decisions about what we want and don't want, we begin to reason and question, to use our own mind rather than believing in and doing things just because our parents or someone else said so. Most children in Western societies are not taught nor encouraged to study the modalities that give insight into our blueprints. Imagine how much easier life could be if from a young age we learned to understand our chosen journey. We may not like some of what potentially lies ahead of us, but we would be in a much better position to master the challenges when they arise, before they become big issues. It may also be easier to accept the hardships at ego level if we realize that they have a higher purpose or are meant to awaken us to a greater spiritual truth about ourselves.

Studying our blueprint is not likely to tell us everything there is to know about ourselves, although it will provide great insight into the purpose of the life we have chosen and why we are the person we are. If we are going to study our personality and the negatives in our life, then it is very beneficial to practise seeing our situations from the perspective that there are levels of truth, as this is much more productive than seeing life from a "right or wrong" perspective. We also need to remember that our perceptions and personal truths are influenced by our LTM-based core beliefs. We had no control over the data we downloaded, because we were too young to know any better. But as we grow up, we claim the data as our own and then we identify our self-worth with it, even though we did not create it, so we don't need to own it. We can always be open to the possibility that there may be higher truths out there.

Money, power, and the desire for material possessions take a back seat when the driver is seeking spiritual growth. These things are not bad, but unlike our ego self, our spirit is not so tempted by them. The ego self generally wants to enjoy life with the least amount of effort and pain possible. Money and power create security while material possessions create comfort and enjoyment. There is nothing wrong with wanting these things, but it can become a problem when the ego wants them more than it needs them. An extreme example of this is how and why the rich keep getting richer. Their needs were filled long ago but they keep wanting more, and for many wealth has become associated with power. Power creates security. However, the ego will die and its needs will cease to be. The spirit wants happiness and inner peace along with greater spiritual awareness, and anything gained in these areas will go with it after the death of the physical self. One of the greatest rewards for becoming more spiritually aware is that we have our awareness for eternity. We don't lose our level of consciousness when we die. We take it with us.

EXERCISE 10: MEASURING DESIRES

This exercise is intended to measure your spirit- and ego-based desires. Be honest with yourself as you complete the following steps:

1. Think about what you want to do in this lifetime.
2. Write a list of ten (or more) things you would like to achieve before you die.
3. Reflect on how important each one is to you and number them in order of importance from 1 to 10, and so on.
4. Next to each item, note whether it is a spirit or an ego desire. If both apply, consider it a spirit-driven want.

This is a great way to measure how keen you are about your spiritual journey and how important your ego wants and desires are to you. Ask yourself the following questions:

1. How balanced is your list?
2. Are your ego desires interfering with your spirit desires?

3. Do you want to change any items or the order of your list, and if so, how prepared are you to make the change?
4. What ego desires are you prepared to let go of if they interfere with your spirit goals? Evaluate how committed you are to your spiritual journey and if you need to change any ego-based desires that might be interfering with your spiritual life.

We cannot have it both ways, and our ego desires can sabotage our spiritual journey, if we let them. If you want to test that belief, then try to give up something that your ego really enjoys but is not good for you. As you know, changing our beliefs often takes commitment and persistence. It is the same with our desires.

Right and wrong belong in an old paradigm. Levels of truth belong in a new one. Nobody is right or wrong anymore. We are all living from and expressing our level of truth. As our consciousness expands, so does our ability to see a bigger picture. Bigger pictures hold higher truths. Everybody is doing the best that they can from their level of consciousness. We are encouraged to grow by inspiration and discouraged by criticism. Nearly everyone wants to be liked and to feel safe. Unfortunately, this desire has also created one of our greatest forms of self-deception—the higher self mask.

10

Images and the Higher Self Mask

THIS CHAPTER is about how we create the images of self. An image is how we present ourselves to the world or how we want the world to see us; for example, as a nice person, happy, calm, loving, composed, successful, tough, superior, victimized, unlucky, helpless, and so on. We develop these images to attract different forms of love and power, ultimately to feel safe. You may also present yourself in a way that portrays a stronger quality than you actually have or that you don't have at all. An image is used to cover up a part of you that you don't want people to see. This false presentation results from a want, and in relation to others, this "pseudo you" has conditions attached. The real you, however, has no conditions, because it doesn't want anything in return. It's not easy for others to discern between our images and our real selves, but one is manipulative and insincere while the other is naturally honest and sincere.

Let us presume that you are a naturally happy person most of the time. Now imagine that your day at the office is not going well and you are feeling angry. A colleague approaches you for a chat and you don't want to let her see that you are angry. You put on a big smile and it's easy to do, because you're good at being happy. But this happy face is not genuine. It is the result of an intention to project an image or mask of a happy person in a moment when you are unhappy. Why would you do that? What is the gain? The answer may be that your pride does not want to people to see that you are angry; you might view your anger as a weakness and feel aversion to exposing it; you might like the positive attention you get from always being happy, and so on. In any case, you receive a gain from projecting a happy image.

People often do seemingly genuine, unconditional acts with the intention of wanting something in return. Such an action or gesture comes from someone wearing a higher self mask. They have selfish intentions and their aim is to "hook you in" or to "win you over," in the worst scenarios with devious intentions. Another common expression used to justify personal gain at someone else's expense is, "The end justifies the means." This implies that a person will do what they will to get what they want, and any collateral damage incurred is secondary. This seems to be common practice in today's society, with pervasive dishonesty as the collateral damage of so many pursuing their own selfish desires. This problem is rife in most areas, including politics and big business.

LEARNING TO CREATE IMAGES

Children will learn to suppress a negative and express a positive to get the outcomes they want. For example, they may suppress their feelings of hurt and pretend to be happy or quash their anger to a point where they show no emotion at all. Another example is how boys have been taught to withhold tears. Up until recently, a prevalent saying was, "Big boys don't cry." Crying was not considered manly. This inadvertently steered many older boys into showing very few emotions at all. One unforeseen outcome was that many men learnt to suppress nearly all their emotions, including those associated with love.

It is natural to want to survive. Even as babies and young children, we will do whatever it takes to stay alive. Infants learn very quickly, mainly by observing what happens around them. When they experience anger, they feel fearful and unsafe; when they experience love and happiness, they feel safe. They are vulnerable to emotional hurt until they become wise to the harsh reality of how tough life can be. The innocence of a child's thought processes quickly dissipates as they learn to do what they need to do to feel safe.

A young child reacts when they feel emotionally hurt. Their first reaction may be to cry, sulk, or express anger or any other raw emotion. These expressions are mostly natural and unconditional because the child does not know how to use them for any self-gain. These raw reactions last until babies learn otherwise. The majority of babies and young children who develop in a safe, loving environment tend to grow up being calm, trusting, and open, while those who grow up in emotionally or physically unsafe environments are more likely to be nervous, angry, aggressive, or very defensive.

For an infant in an environment causing distress, if the reaction is understood and honoured and they feel supported and loved, the child will learn that it is safe to express their true self. However, when an infant does not feel supported by the parent in a moment of distress, they feel unsafe. If the infant feels unsafe some or all of the time, then their natural instincts for survival will take over and they will adapt by developing a reaction that makes them feel safe, most likely modifying behaviour. When the child's original reaction does not serve them because it creates an unsafe environment, they try to control that reaction or stop doing it. The child learns to suppress their natural reaction, finding one more conducive to a loving response—and their only judgement is about whether the modified behaviour works. Does it create a safe environment? If so, the reaction is good and if not, it is bad.

For example, an innocent child breaks something and runs to tell a parent about it. It happens that the object was precious, and the parent gives the child a reprimand or, in the worst-case scenario, a severe punishment. The child did not mean to break the object, but there was still trouble for being honest. The result is the child felt much unloved and unsafe. The child concludes that telling the truth is unsafe and modifies the behaviour to create a safer outcome. The next time something is broken, the child hides the pieces of evidence and doesn't tell the parent. He or she may be scared about getting into trouble if found out but decide it's worth the risk because it is better than the fear that resulted previously from being honest. Children will often tell a lie and then worry about being found out. They may want to own up but are too scared of the consequences. Lies often create guilt and so the children feel bad and may continue to feel unsafe. This is bad for self-esteem. It is normally very hard to admit a lie once it is told, and so they start to develop little secrets about some of the things they have done. We all carry the legacy that comes from telling lies in our early childhood.

We all have consciences that challenge us to admit to lies. In the example above, what can the child do? She or he can own up and tell the truth, but that could bring a lot more trouble and may put her or his safety in jeopardy. To keep the secret will cause feelings of guilt, which creates a very negative mental state. Two ways of overcoming guilt are to either own up to the cause or suppress the memory of the situation. Many children and adults would rather not admit to something they did if doing so would get them into trouble. An easier option is to avoid telling the truth (in other words, lie) and then suppress the guilt. Continual suppression will train children's brains to tamp down the memory so deeply in the subconscious that they will forget about the original issue. Suppression is normally achieved by avoiding thinking or speaking about something, and that is a form of denial. Many of our most emotionally painful memories are hidden in our subconscious, some so deeply that it takes a skilled therapist to help us remember them.

A Note on Suppression

I have worked with people who have been horrifically abused. In some cases, they have come for therapy to deal with an issue seemingly unrelated to the abuse, but as we work towards the core of their issue, they have minor flashbacks. It is often a delicate, slow process as the memories are recalled. I have noticed that the mind will sometimes only allow us to see little pieces of the picture to begin with, because too much exposure would probably send the person into shock, and I have never seen people receive a bigger flashback than they can handle. Once, over several sessions, the full picture is exposed, they are ready to heal to the level that they require. Core beliefs are never fully removed, but their associated energy can be completely healed or transmuted and so their effects lose impact.

I have huge respect for our ability to suppress very painful memories. The only way that I know how to uncover deeply buried memories that create core beliefs is to see how they show up in certain patterns in a person's life. These core beliefs reveal themselves through sublime patterns that discolour a person's experiences.

When, as children, people are too scared to share their stories because of the potential humiliation and fear of not being believed, that developing attitude can become strong enough to form a core belief. Once a core belief, it will keep playing itself out until they feel safe enough to tell someone trustworthy about it.

The subconscious guilt will still generate negative energy. This negative thought pattern will create future outcomes but a person suppressing a memory will not be aware of what causes the outcomes. Unless the negative pattern is healed or transmuted, then these manifestations will keep developing. Sometimes the outcomes don't show up for many years, making it difficult to connect the original issue to how it has manifested.

Images and Talents

Another ingredient can be added to the cocktail of our images, having to do with our natural talents and gifts. We all have better and worse aspects of our personality and abilities. The better is what comes naturally to us—what we are good at without trying. We act out these talents or (so-called) gifts with little or no effort and often without intending to do so. They are automatic and unconditional. We enact them without thought of reward such as acknowledgement, appreciation, or compensation. We do what we do because we are what we are. We may offer someone love and compassion because we naturally feel their pain or relate to their situation. A mother may protect and nurture her baby because doing so is innate to her and there is no thought of anything in return. It feels good to give and that giving does not need to be appreciated or acknowledged.

Imagine a young boy who often reacted with anger and always got punished by a parent for doing so. He eventually learnt to suppress that anger and turned to one of his natural gifts to gain the parent's love, to feel safe. Let's presume that, because he mastered being loving in a past life, he had a lovable personality. He suppressed his anger-based behaviour and modified it, because when he put on the charm he found that he was able to win back his parent's love. He soon learnt that his charm was a real asset. What has he done here? He turned a natural, unconditional act of being lovable and charming into one that got a reward. He then knew that he could use his charm to get love in this world, to win people's friendship or perhaps whatever he wanted. He could use this natural gift to manipulate people or avoid conflict. When he expressed it in its natural state, his loving personality was unconditional, and when he used the same charm for gain, it became conditional. Children quickly learn that their gifts can be very powerful qualities that keep them safe and get them what they want.

On the receiving end, people usually aren't able to tell if an action is conditional or unconditional. Charm is often perceived as genuine when it may be manipulative and deceptive. A non-genuine act is from an image that people use to get something they want. It is often just as confusing for the person projecting the image, because they won't clearly see what they are doing.

Such deception can only come from the lower self, because negatives do not exist in the higher self. People consciously or unconsciously use positive qualities for a hidden negative purpose—to gain something in return. A lower-self intention masquerading as a higher self quality is called a higher self mask. Many people get hurt by this quite unexpected, negative deception and don't understand why or how they've been misled. If they were to discover what's really going on, then in the future they probably would be skeptical about trusting the person who wears the higher self mask. Hurting other people is bad enough, but people wearing the higher self mask usually don't realize that they're doing a lot of damage to their own energy field, too. They not only suppress a negative, which will create disharmony within, but they may also create sickness that could develop into a terminal illness. They also delude themselves, thinking they are nice, good people when they are actually lying to themselves and others every time they wear their higher self mask.

Generally, wearers of the higher self mask will push people away. Humans naturally like one another but they are also naturally repelled by negative energy. They will look for the positives in people and try to ignore any negative energy that others radiate. However, deep down they innately sense this negative energy and a part of them is repulsed by it. Their mind may be telling them to like the person while their intuition indicates that something is not right.

When we see only the best in people, we're not necessarily seeing the whole person. We may deliberately avoid looking for bad qualities in people and likewise ignore our intuition telling us someone is not all good. We have to be very alert to recognize a higher self mask. Too many people are conned out of large amounts of money and possessions because they have not trained themselves to see the whole person. Con artists will prey on this vulnerability until people learn to better discern the real personalities of others, recognizing when someone is wearing a higher self mask. Most con artists have charming higher self masks that seem genuine, making it hard to believe that a dark ulterior motive lurks behind it.

We can also be totally unaware of how we create the negatives with higher self masks in our own life. If we're wearing one, we may get good results, initially, because our ulterior motives aren't clear to others and we don't think we're doing anything wrong. But others will start to see through our mask and eventually withdraw from being our friend. In such situations, often people blame others for the friendship's breakdown because they cannot see their contribution to the outcome.

EXERCISE 11: DISCERNING ACTION

This exercise is to help you discern whether an act is genuine or motivated by an outcome (in other words, an image-based act):

1. Recall an action that you took recently. For example, it could be doing a favour for a friend, an interaction you had at work, a kind word you said to your partner, and so on.
2. Reflect on whether you were seeking a response based on your action. What was your reaction to the response (or non-response)?

If you received a negative response and you felt hurt, know that you had a condition attached to your action. For example, the image of you as a helpful person was not met with appreciation. If you received a positive response, then it may be your image achieved its purpose. If, during your action, you expected a response, know that you were acting out an image and wanted something in return. A genuine, totally unconditional action does not require or look for anything in return. You may even be surprised by a response because you were not expecting it. For example, you say something kind to someone and she thanks you. If your act was coming from your true self, you may feel surprised by the gratitude because you were acting unconditionally.

Suppressed Emotions

Another function of images is to draw focus away from suppressed negative emotions. For example, you could be so preoccupied with helping someone that you don't notice you're angry because you feel obligated to help. This anger accrues with an associated emotion from a childhood situation in which you felt you had no choice, and subconsciously the energy of anger builds, creating negative outcomes. Although at first they may not be apparent, eventually the outcomes will be obvious.

In such a situation, you may be generating two energies at the same time by consciously doing something and unconsciously projecting a higher self mask, hoping to get something in return. You believe the conscious action is a positive energy, but it is really coming from a negative ulterior motive. It often requires a high level of self-awareness to be able to recognize the truth in situations because of the many contributing factors. Eventually this type of image will come back to bite you, if not right away then eventually, because the natural cycles of energy guarantee it. One of the longer-term outcomes can be that the energy of the anger will eventually build to an amplitude strong enough to cause emotional and physical disharmony that often manifests into disease. All that negative energy has an effect on your cells.

The following chart shows how the process of the higher self mask unfolds.

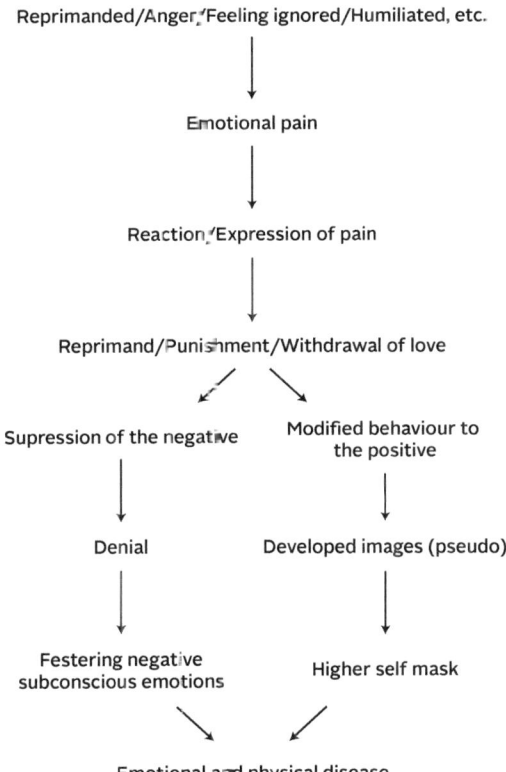

As the chart above shows, childhood wounds can eventually lead to emotional and physical disease. For example, when babies or very young children experience negatives, such as being reprimanded or the target of anger, neglect, humiliation, and so on, they experience emotional pain and react by expressing it.

If they experience further negativity, such as a parent's anger, reprimand, or punishment, then they experience the withdrawal of that parent's love and they feel unsafe, so they tend to do two things. They learn to suppress their pain and to modify their behaviour to win back their parent's love.

However, if their initial reaction is honoured by the parent and the children feel safe, then this issue normally stops there.

If children repeatedly suppress the negative, then it will move into their subconscious where it covertly generates negative energy. As adults, they may deny that they have or ever had a problem. However, festering negative energy accrues similar energy until it becomes strong enough to create outcomes that show up in the personality or even as sickness in the body.

Meanwhile, modified behaviour generates a positive energy designed to substitute for the real reaction, which was negative.

In modifying behaviour, usually a quality that garners a positive reaction, such as love, is chosen to enact. A modified behaviour becomes an image when it is used to gain something back. This image is a mask that covers up a negative. The mask eventually becomes a higher self mask, which is a mask of the worst kind and contributes to the potential of emotional and physical disease, because it diverts awareness away from the festering negative caused by the initial wound.

THE CHART ON the previous page shows a very powerful example of the psychosomatic principle in action (a pain in the mind creates a pain in the body). A psychosomatic outcome is ultimately positive from a spiritual point of view. It alerts us to a negative energy that we have not processed so that we can positively deal with it on both a physical and a spiritual level. If we are experiencing emotional pain on a physical level, then we know that we are also experiencing it on a spiritual level as well. Any negative energy that we hold in our field will have an effect on our overall vibration and thus slow our spiritual evolution down.

II
Moving Through the Third Dimension

· · · · · · ·

THIS BOOK has provided a model of how the super consciousness that I call God came into being and how aspects of It created the universe and then gave life to all within it. The universe functions as a whole consciousness governed by the universal laws. Everything is a form of energy and if we understand the principles that govern energy, then we will come to know an aspect of God. Humans have a relationship to all creation through the hologram principle and we are a small but integral part of the greater whole. We have also examined how the one universal mind is aligned with but separate from the mind of the Creator. All forms of creation can access the universal mind and have the potential to communicate with all other forms through this one mind. We have also explored what is activated when we make choices about who we are and what we want to create. Now we will consider how we apply these principles to improving our lives and how we use them to elevate our consciousness.

The information offered in this book can help us understand how we can evolve through the experiences of the earth plane and find the permanent inner peace that we desire. We can also speed up the completion of the different cycles of experience we call life on earth. One thing is certain: Everything in creation is a form of energy and, therefore, it will naturally return to the point of its creation. We cannot avoid returning to our source, which is God, because it is inevitable. We have a choice about how long it takes to return to the "God state" found in the Oneness; nevertheless, there is no time limit for mastering the experiences of the third dimension. How long it takes is up to us and the choices we make. There is no way out and there are no easy shortcuts. We cannot get off the train to enlightenment. We can resist the cycle with all our might, but the nature of the cycle will eventually bring us to a point where our awareness will master the experiences provided in the third dimension.

We ignore or reject the universal laws at our own peril. The level of consciousness of many humans does not allow them to understand the seriousness and the consequences of the choices they have made in the past and are making now. The priority of most is to seek happiness and safety rather than inner peace and higher consciousness. Most of us just want to enjoy life and do it in the easiest way possible. However, avoiding the higher truths won't make them go away and only makes the journey harder. We can only make choices and create in the present moment, because the past is gone and the future has not arrived yet. We can only focus on our current reality of mastering the third-dimension experiences. We may want to live in the spirit world or the future, but our current reality is embedded in the physical and so this is the plane of consciousness where we can manifest change.

We cannot skip over a part of the journey that we don't enjoy. There is only one way out, and that is upwards. Any other direction will direct us further towards where we don't want to be. The only way to stop the cycle of reincarnation is by raising our vibration to a level that is in sync with a vibration of a higher dimension. We can either keep raising our vibration or keep reincarnating. If we want to keep returning to the third dimension, we don't have to raise our vibration. But we can choose to master the challenges provided by the earth plane to climb to a higher dimension.

This next reality is probably the most painful one to face in the third dimension: We are entirely responsible for our experiences. The first step to freedom from the state we are in is to realize that we created it in the first place. When we own that we alone have created our situation, we have the power to change it. Changing our reality requires effort, commitment, discipline, and vigilance, continuously making higher choices along with numerous realizations, self-forgiveness, and the release of any guilt and karma that we carry. One of the best preparations for this journey is to understand that to seek the unity with the whole, we have to realize that separation and unity are opposites. We are either one or the other, because the two cannot co-exist. We cannot aim to return to God and hold on to the perceived freedom that comes with individuality. Many humans may like the concept of attaining higher levels of consciousness; however, they are very reluctant to let go of the beliefs and possessions that hold them back.

One misconception is that we have to give up the power and freedom associated with being an individual. If we believe that we must give up something, then it is likely to cause stress; the survival instincts of our first brain activate, perceiving change as a threat, and so resistance sets in. When we climb higher, we let go of something because we no longer need it, and we only do that when we are ready. We need to be inspired or at least enthusiastic about the journey. If we know where we are heading in the long run, then it is easier to stay focused. We need to understand our goal and be clear in our mind about what we want.

Transitioning to the spiritual path is not easy; it is generally a slow, step-by-step process with moments of inspiration and encouragement from the higher levels of consciousness. The rewards may be subtle, but in spiritual terms they are huge. We must activate the love in our heart on this journey because love's vibration is what opens up the doorways to the higher planes of consciousness. It is helpful to remember that the higher planes are always sending us information and help through the universal mind, whether or not we are aware of it. It is up to us to tune into it.

When the heart is involved, it generates the love energy that amplifies the desire to be part of the Oneness. The energy goes out to the universe and comes back with a lot more power. Some spiritual teachings say it comes back ten times stronger. It is easy to see that we are not alone on this journey when we have support like that. This is why our intention is so important. We need clear intentions because the universe will respond likewise but with much more power. If we keep changing our mind and send out confused or contradictory intentions, then we can expect the universe to respond in kind. We are likely to become more confused and contradictory and get lost if we always change our direction. We have to be responsible for our thoughts and actions because the higher we climb, the more powerful our thoughts and actions become. This means that we will create more powerful outcomes. The positive outcomes will in turn speed up our spiritual climb.

That we have created our current situations may sound like doom and gloom for some people because it exposes us to the reality of the consequences of our past actions and choices.

There is a shining light that penetrates that gloom: We cannot fail but to return back to the light of God because it is impossible not to. Ask yourself this: "What do I want to do with my life? Do I want spiritual freedom or do I want to do what I have always done?" Focus must shift from the pleasures of the physical world to the requirements of the spirit. We don't have to give up our worldly possessions, but we need to give up our love for them. If we put the love of money before our desire to spiritually evolve, then that is enough to keep us in the cycles of reincarnation. We may be able to fool ourselves and others that we have the highest intentions but we cannot fool the universe, because our true inner beliefs, desires, and secrets create their own vibrations. Our personal truth cannot hide from the highest levels of consciousness, because the universe reads our vibrations, not our actions.

CLIMBING THROUGH DIMENSIONS

The higher we climb through the dimensions, the higher and lighter the vibrations become and there is less resistance. Some models stipulate that there are ten dimensions or planes of awareness that we pass through on our way back to the Oneness. The first dimension is the lowest vibrating, making it the densest, with the most resistance. Some information suggests that we have already passed through the first and second dimensions, where we had only experience because we had no choice or free will. We are now experiencing the third dimension of the earth plane of choice and free will. It is also a dimension on the lower end of the consciousness scale, which means the vibration of its energy is slower and, therefore, it is denser than the higher dimensions. Density creates resistance; therefore, this is a plane of great resistance, and the greater the resistance, the greater the effort required to pass through it. We all face this reality when trying to overcome our greatest challenges. Some channelled information suggests that this is the most challenging of all the dimensions and that any changes that happen in this dimension have a huge effect on the other dimensions simply because of the high amplitudes of energy required to implement change. We know that all energy affects all other energy, and the greater the amount of energy involved, the bigger the effect.

If we want to spiritually evolve, then we have to push through the resistance and not take the easy path. The further we move along the road less travelled, the more personal and self-reliant our journey becomes, because we will encounter fewer people on the same level of consciousness. The further we travel, the less others will be able to relate to us, and so it can become very lonely if we rely on our interactions with others to make us happy. Happiness has to be generated from within and this becomes a natural flow once we really connect with the higher dimensions. When the negativity of the third dimension has less effect on us, one of the rewards is inner peace. It is also very empowering not to be affected by the world around us. Anyone who has reached mastery has this ability.

What Do You Want to Do?

A decision to make a positive effort will increase your vibration. Denial, avoidance, indecision, no decision, negative decisions, and seemingly positive decisions with negative intentions will all eventually create a living hell if they are not addressed. If we do not align with the choices made by our spirit (in the blueprint), then our life will be much harder than it needs to be.

Hell is not a punishment—it is an outcome! It seems that the ego has only one sensible choice and that is to move towards becoming more aware while working within the boundaries of the blueprint. All the ego really does is make decisions that make life as easy as it can be or harder than it needs to be. God cares about us but does not interfere with our decisions. It observes and experiences the outcomes with us. If we connect with the higher consciousness, then we can gain Its support. If we want to experience separation and individuality, then we can and we still have God's support, which raises the question again, "What do you want to do?"

If you want to connect with the higher vibrations, then here is some information that will help guide you. These are key elements of the journey forward, some of which you may have already made decisions about:

- Come to terms with the reality that you are the only one responsible for everything in your life. You have created it all and, therefore, you also are the only one in charge of changing it.
- Stop blaming, because it sabotages your ability to take responsibility for what happens in your life.
- Learn to control your thoughts, because your thoughts create your future. This is an ongoing activity.
- Embrace that there are levels of truth and let go of any attachment to the opposing polarities of right and wrong, good and bad, and so on, because you are moving into a higher consciousness where everything simply is.
- Do not identify your self-worth with what you believe.
- Practise letting go of judgement about spiritual matters. Judgement does not exist on the higher planes of consciousness; it is replaced with understanding, love, and compassion.
- Work towards having the faith that you cannot fail to return to your source. All you can really do is shorten or lengthen the length of the cycle of reincarnation that you

are continuously affecting with your everyday thoughts and actions.
- Know that as you work towards having more faith, your fear slowly but surely dissipates.
- Believe that the rewards for your efforts will be tenfold, because you activate the support of the universe when you set an intention and act on it.
- Be aware that the universe responds to your intentions and what's in your heart, not your requests, wants, or actions. Prayer and meditation without these two ingredients will be lacking and may not create what you want.
- Know that what you create is an expression of your thoughts and deeper intentions. If your thoughts have pure intentions, then your creation will be an expression of that. Likewise, if your thoughts and intention are devious, then you will create a negative outcome. Look to the outcomes to discover your inner truth.
- Understand that thought and emotion have a powerful effect on the vibration of your energy field. Thoughts affect your heart, which generates your emotions. Purify your thoughts and you will purify the love that is generated in your heart.
- Accept that the love generated by your heart has by far the greatest effect on your vibration. This is why it is said that the way to God is through love.
- Be aware that our journey into higher consciousness is subject to the creative process of thought, word, and deed. We have an original thought about how we will move forward. We think about what we will do. We act it out by applying it to life. We can then reflect on the outcome and decide what we want to do next, gaining wisdom as we do.
- Know that the road ahead is not meant to be easy, because you cannot attain mastery if there is nothing to challenge you.

- Understand that there are no miracles, luck, or coincidences. These are merely terms that explain the seemingly inexplicable. All outcomes are the results of some form of creative consciousness.

You are evolving towards a place of unimaginable peace and beauty. It is up to you to decide what you want to do now. It always has been.

Putting Study into Practice
We will not directly evolve by studying something. To activate the process of creation and experience teachings requires action. We come to know truth through experience. If the process has a positive effect on our consciousness, we will evolve a little further. If not, then we need not endorse that information.

Our life is our greatest teacher. We are very wise if we learn from what life presents us. After all, our blueprint guides our life and, therefore, it has a huge effect on what we experience. We are complex beings with the potential to be incredibly powerful creators. We have to get to know ourselves on a very deep level if we want to realize that potential.

Keep in mind that life is made up of experiences designed for us to learn the lessons we need. We progress through the school of life in the same way that we progress through our education system. Every year of study is designed to prepare us for the next grade. If we don't master the lower grades, we won't be successful at the higher ones. When we graduate from school, we participate in the workforce, where we apply the knowledge we gained. Some of what we learned is useful, and some is not. When we engage in life after school, then we use what's beneficial and discard the rest.

The school of life is the same. We start at the bottom and work our way up through the levels of awareness, mastering one level at a time. We cannot fool the universe about the level we are on because our consciousness generates vibrations that the universe reads. We cannot rush the lessons. It takes time and patience, so we might as well go with the flow that our blueprint provides us and enjoy the journey as much as we can.

Here are the main ways that we can get to know ourselves and speed up our spiritual journey:

- Study the universal laws and learn to live by them.
- Attain as much information about our blueprint as we can.
- Study our personality.
- Observe what we think about and how we act and react.
- Apply huge doses of self-honesty. The truth will help free us from our past and pave the way for a better future.
- Learn to generate the love energy from our heart.

If you become familiar with and apply the wisdom gained from the subjects above, you will speed up your spiritual journey through the third dimension.

There are several versions of the universal laws, and it is beneficial to read them all to gain the most information and wisdom that you can. Although this book has not directly addressed the universal laws, they have had a great influence on the truths found in it. In addition to what has been touched on in this book, much information about the universal laws can be found online; for example, at https://intuerifarm.files.wordpress.com/2013/09/the-12-universal-laws.pdf and www.nofearliving.com.

Many books and courses on self-awareness and self-improvement are available. Some will suit you and others may even leave you feeling like you have been misled by egotistical charlatans. You will be inspired by the courses that are right for you. Not all the courses and information available will suit you, so do due diligence before investing time, money, or other energy into anything. Having said that, nothing is lost no matter what you read or experience, so long as you are prepared to learn from it. Sometimes we do things that help us determine what we want and don't want. Some of our greatest negative experiences provide us with some of our best lessons. Emotional pain can be a great wake-up call, if becoming aware is what you require.

Many people will have advice about what they think is best for you. Take it as advice only. They mainly base that information on their own experiences. Nobody can tell you what is right for your spiritual journey, because they cannot read your blueprint. What is in your astrology and numerology charts, along with your palm readings, will give you a guide but not all the answers. One of the greatest tools for working out what is right for you is your power of discernment. You can take information in and reflect on it afterwards, making an informed judgement. It has to make sense to you. Do not believe it just because somebody says it is the truth or that it is right. It is the same with everything: The more you practise discernment, the more proficient you will become with it.

Psychosomatics is the study of the relationship between the mind and the body. The energy of our thoughts manifests in and through our body. It is one way that we can uncover very negative conscious and subconscious beliefs. There is a well-known correlation between the mind and health. We can identify negative belief systems and thought patterns by tracking how they affect the body. Louise Hay wrote several books on the relationship between our negative beliefs and thoughts and how they manifest in our body in the form of sickness and disease.

Once you understand why you are who you are and what you have come to achieve, you can target the areas of your life that need attention and change. After gaining knowledge and understanding, you must apply it to life; otherwise, the information will be merely a concept. The hardest part of spiritual growth is uncovering our deepest negatives and applying the change required to increase our vibration.

12

The God State

A NYTHING THAT is created can only ever be a creation and cannot be its creator. The spiritual teaching that says we were created in the likeness of God explains that we cannot be God, but we can communicate with God or be in God's presence. Through the universal mind, we communicate with God. The Creator's mind and the universal mind communicate with each other. We can communicate with God via this connection of minds. When we learn to separate our self from the mind, we can be in the presence of God. Consciousness can be measured by its vibration. God has a vibration. We have the potential to increase our vibration to a level where we can be in God's presence. It is like being in the same room as God. This is totally different to communicating through prayer, which is more like talking to God on the telephone.

Each level of our consciousness can communicate only with the level above it. Our physical or ego self is the lowest level and it can communicate with our spirit self. The spirit self communicates with the next level, which is the higher self, including everything above the imaginary line of separation discussed in Chapter 7. Therefore, it is our spirit self, not the ego, that can connect with the highest levels of consciousness, which includes God.

The more time we spend in our higher self, the more familiar we will become with these higher aspects. We also become aware of the "I AM" state. We can achieve the I AM state when we are in deep meditation, and this allows us to be in God's presence. All this means that we need to have the awareness that takes our vibration above the line. If we understand that we are a part of the whole, then we may be in the presence of any part of the whole, including God. If we believe that we are separate from the whole, then our awareness will reflect that belief. This perceived separation will restrict us to communicating with the whole instead of being in its presence. This is a critical point, because it distinguishes our ability to be in God's presence. It is much easier to separate our self from the mind once our consciousness evolves to the higher self awareness that exists above the line.

ACCESSING THE GOD STATE

Brain-Rhythm Cycles

There are several different models on the Internet that describe the brainwaves related to different states of consciousness. The busiest state of consciousness in this model is the beta state and the most relaxed is the delta state. The various states create correlated frequencies of brainwaves (measured in hertz per second). These frequencies are also known as brain-rhythm cycles. The chart that follows is a general presentation based on various representations. It is not meant to be a precise model, but is intended to give you an idea of the relationship between the levels of consciousness and our brainwaves.

Levels of consciousness	Brain wave frequency/ Brain rhythm cycles per second
Beta	14–30
Alpha	8–14
Theta	4–8
Delta	0–4
God state	minus 10 (1 cycle every 10 seconds)

A Note about the God State

The information that contributed to my awareness of the God state of consciousness came in pieces, during different deep meditations, during which I had out-of-body experiences. The story unfolded during specific meditations that I practised sporadically. It took many years for all the pieces to fall into place and for the story to come together.

I learnt to meditate during my early thirties. I gained good skills that got me into the delta state. I eventually noticed a strange rocking sensation that started in my head. I allowed it to develop and it spread throughout my body. The rocking became so strong that I felt like I would fall out of my chair. I asked someone to observe me during this state and they said that I did not move at all. It was very strange. During one of these deep meditations, I was told that I was experiencing brain-rhythm cycles and instructed to slow them down to one beat every ten seconds. I was able to do this because I could feel each cycle. When I was in this state many years later, a voice told me that this was the God state. I don't know what voice it was or where it came from, but it had authority. I kept this in my memory, but I still did not understand what was being shown to me. Many years later, I was meditating to access my Akashic records. On the third visit, I was met by my guides and taken to a place where I passed through a glass door. I knew that I was in the state of minus 10 (1 cycle per 10 seconds). Again, I was told that this was the God state. Though I responded by saying that this was blasphemous, as I cannot be in a God state, my guides told me that blasphemy is only of the ego/physical self, and I had symbolically left that behind when I'd passed through the glass door. A few days later I pieced the story together. Deep meditations require us to separate ourselves from our mind. This allows our higher self to be in charge. This then prepares the way for us to access the God state. The spirit self has to first have the awareness that it is a part of the whole, which elevates its consciousness above the line of separation into the realm of the higher self and all that is. I believe that this higher awareness is a prerequisite that enables the experience of the God state.

I have never taught anyone how to reach this state but I have no doubt that it was shown to me so that I could share it. It takes a lot of concentration to get into this state and it is even harder to hold. I believe that it is attained by first setting the intention and concentrating on relaxing deeply into the meditative state. (You may be able to tune in to the pulses of the brain-rhythm cycles. These can be felt in and around the brain.) I am not sure whether I do the accessing or I am taken into the God state. Either way, it is a great privilege. It is the state of being in the presence of God. Sometimes, I have thought about questions that I would like to ask before I go into this state. However, the questions just seem irrelevant and pointless once I am there. It is as though I already know the answers, so there is no point in asking. There is nothing to do or say in this state. When you reach it, just be!

MOVING UPWARDS

The journey through the third dimension into higher consciousness is so personal that no one can tell you how to master your unique path. All anyone can do is offer you information to guide you. Be very wary of anyone who says, "Follow me, I know the way for you." They may know how they did it, but they can only provide you with information to help you find your way. Your enlightenment is a state of consciousness that only you can find, because it is hidden within.

May you find and follow your path with passion.
You are the creator and master of your own destiny!

Conclusion

. . . .

THIS BOOK is a part of an ongoing story. My never-ending search for more understanding and answers to the questions about the purpose of life and the conscious evolution of our spirit will no doubt lead me to sharing more information as the bigger picture unfolds. Please visit my website to keep in touch: davidlane.net.au.

I am a great believer that everyone, once given the tools to do so, can find and master his or her unique path into higher consciousness.

Enjoy your journey!

DAVID LANE

Resources

• • • • • • •

THE CONCEPTS presented in this book are the result of information drawn from a variety of beliefs and teachings that I have explored for nearly six decades. I have been influenced by many spiritual teachers, scientists, and authors in this journey seeking a higher understanding of the purpose of life. Here is a list of those who have had the most influence on my thoughts about how we evolve our consciousness.

Braden, Gregg S. *Awakening to Zero Point: The Collective Initiation.* Radio Bookstore Press, 1997.

Brennan, Barbara Ann. *Hands of Light: A Guide to Healing Through the Human Energy Field.* Bantam Books, 1988.

Cannon, Delores. *Jesus and The Essenes.* Gateway Books, 1992.

———. *The Convoluted Universe* (series). Ozark Mountain Publishing, Inc., 2001.

Childre, Doc, and Howard Martin. *The HeartMath Solution: The Institute of HeartMath's Revolutionary Program for Engaging the Power of the Heart's Intelligence.* HarperCollins, 2000.

Chopra, Deepak. *Ageless Body, Timeless Mind: A Practical Alternative to Growing Old*. Random House, 1993.

Dychtwald, Ken. *Bodymind*. Pantheon Books, 1977.

Hay, Louise. *You Can Heal Your Life*. Hay House, 2004.

Howard, Vernon. *The Mystic Path to Cosmic Power*. Parker Publishing Co., 1973.

Krebs, Charles, and Jenny Brown. *A Revolutionary Way of Thinking: From a Near-Fatal Accident to a New Science of Healing*. Hill of Content Publishing Co., 1998.

Lipton, Bruce H. *The Biology of Belief: Unleashing the Power of Consciousness, Matter & Miracles*. Mountain of Love/Elite Books, 2005.

Millman, Dan. *The Life You Were Born to Live: A Guide to Finding Your Life Purpose*. New World Library, 1993.

Myss, Carolyn. *Invisible Acts of Power: The Divine Energy of a Giving Heart*. Simon & Schuster, 2004.

Peale, Norman Vincent. *The Power of Positive Thinking: Ten Traits for Maximum Results*. Cedar Book, 1953.

Pearsall, Paul. *The Heart's Code: Tapping the Wisdom and Power of Our Heart's Energy*. Broadway Books, 1998.

Pert, Candice. *Molecules of Emotion: Why You Feel the Way You Feel*. Scribner, 1997.

Pierrakos, Eva Broch. "The Pathwork Lectures." International Pathwork Foundation. Accessed October 14, 2017. https://pathwork.org/the-lectures/.

———, and Donovan Thesenga. *Fear No Evil: The Pathwork Method of Transforming the Lower Self*. Pathwork Press, 1993.

Reich, Wilhelm. *Character Analysis*. Translated by Mary Boyd Higgins. Noonday Press, 1990.

Rohr, Richard, and Andreas Ebert. *The Enneagram: A Christian Perspective*. The Crossroad Publishing Company, 2001.

———, and Joseph Martos. *The Wild Man's Journey: Reflections on Male Spirituality*. St. Anthony Messenger Press, 1992.

Thesenga, Susan. *The Undefended Self: Living the Pathwork*. Pathwork Press, 1994.

Tolle, Eckhart. *The Power of Now: A Guide to Spiritual Enlightenment*. Hodder & Stoughton, 2001.

———. *A New Earth: Create a Better Life*. Penguin Group, 2005.

Walsch, Neale Donald. *Conversations with God* (series). Hodder & Stoughton, 1995.

Watson, Lyall. *Beyond Supernature: A New Natural History of the Supernatural*. Hodder & Stoughton, 1986.

www.ingramcontent.com/pod-product-compliance
Ingram Content Group UK Ltd.
Pitfield, Milton Keynes, MK11 3LW, UK
UKHW042003230426
12048UKWH00009B/525